D0869148

# Advanced Criminal Law & Investigation

## John Robert Cencich, J.S.D.
### Editor

The Hague Press International

Copyright © by John Robert Cencich
All rights reserved

Library of Congress Cataloging-in-Publication Data
Cencich, John R., 1957 –
   Advanced Criminal Law & Investigation /John R.
   Cencich (ed.)
   Pages cm (studies in crime and public policy)
   ISBN 978-0-9913293-1-1
      (paperback)
   1. Federal Bureau of Investigation *Law Enforcement
      Bulletin.*
   2. Criminal Law.  3. Criminal investigation.
   3. Forensic science. 5. Crime. I. Title.

Printed in the United States
The Hague Press International
First Edition

# CONTENTS

# INTRODUCTION

By

## John Robert Cencich, J.S.D.

SOLVING CRIMES IS A FASCINATING AND REWARDING experience. Such undertakings incorporate both scientific practice and the "art" of good police work. From my perspective, the most successful detectives, investigators, and special agents quite naturally endeavor to blend these notions into a seamless pursuit to unravel the circumstances of the crime and apprehend the offender.

Criminal investigation has come a long way since the days when master-criminal-turned-detective Eugène François Vidoq founded the Sûreté of France, which was originally a small detective force much like London's Bow Street Runners some 60 years earlier. And how can any student of criminal justice or criminology not know about Professor Cesare Lombroso, the founder of the Italian School of Criminology, whose invaluable contributions to crime-solving are often overlooked because of his anthropological theories relative to the connection between body shapes and criminals.

Today's advances in formal, physical, and social sciences have taken crime-solving into another league altogether. It is the integration of these scientific approaches and the investigator's knowledge, skills, and abilities (the art of police work), that increases crime clearance rates. One important component of the knowledge aspect is the legal branch of social science. In other words, the investigator must have an excellent understanding of the law. Indeed, the criminal law is the very foundation of the criminal justice system. Without it, there would be no crimes, and there would be no police, courts, or corrections for two principal reasons.

First, there would be no substantive criminal law, which translates into there being no crimes. In this book we will examine, analyze, and discuss various substantive criminal statutes, which relate to hate crimes, gangs, organized crime, human trafficking, and cold case homicides and sexual assaults. Second, there would be no procedural criminal laws, which regulate how crimes are investigated and prosecuted, the adjudication by the courts, and the penal institutions and their collateral aspects such as probation and parole.

Going beyond the law, what comes to mind when the entire notion of "advanced criminal investigation" comes into play? Forensic science? Criminal profiling? Or perhaps high-tech surveillance equipment? All of these topics will be covered in this course and in this book. And they will be comingled with the law. For example, it does no good to learn about how to install electronic tracking devices on a suspect's vehicle or shipment if the user does not know the law. Even more important, the improper use of such devices can lead to criminal and civil penalties.

You will also learn about recent developments in forensic sciences, and how they can be used in a number of ways including the resolution of cold case homicides and sexual assaults. Adding to this are specialized techniques in the behavioral analysis of violent crime. While very few criminal justice professionals end up becoming full-time "criminal profilers," homicide detectives, sex crimes investigators, and evidence technicians can and do use these skills on a daily basis.

Ultimately, the aim of this book is to lay a foundation for the advanced study of criminal investigation and criminal law. Such an approach is designed to provide a better understanding of complex substantive laws, and the ability to apply this knowledge within the context of procedural criminal law and advanced criminal investigative techniques.

What I have done in this book is taken a number of selected articles that address either U.S. Supreme Court cases or criminal investigation. Most of the relevant articles were drawn from the FBI *Law Enforcement Bulletin* and publications of the National Institute of Justice. They are followed with critical thinking exercises and discussion questions that I developed. To the extent possible, I have interjected my own experiences in the exercises and questions. I will present dilemmas that I have personally been faced with. Sometimes I sorted the issues out, and there were times that I did not. But that is called experience, and there is nothing like personally understanding the struggles that police officers and investigators face on a daily basis and gaining wisdom in the process.

But my experiences are not gratuitous "war stories." I weave my participation and observations into the teaching points. The first objective is to combine reality in regard to the criminal investigative process, with critical thinking and scholarship. This approach is followed by a secondary objective, which is to see how you might respond to some of these situations. Accordingly, we will examine your problem-solving thinking process as an individual, and more import, as part of a team.

John Robert Cencich
Doctor of Juridical Science and
Professor of Criminal Justice

# SUPREME COURT CASES
## 2009-2010 TERM

By Lisa A. Baker, J.D.

November 2010: *FBI Law Enforcement Bulletin*

IN THE MOST RECENT TERM, THE U.S. SUPREME COURT decided several cases of interest to law enforcement. Three addressed legal issues implicated in the taking of statements in criminal investigations. In these cases, the Supreme Court provided additional clarification and guidance concerning the long-standing requirements set forth in *Miranda* v. Arizona, including 1) the circumstances governing when law enforcement may initiate contact with a subject who previously has invoked the *Miranda* right to counsel; 2) what will constitute a waiver of the *Miranda* right to silence; and 3) what must be conveyed to a subject to satisfy *Miranda*.[1]

Another case considered the constitutionality of a warrantless entry into a residence due to concerns about the safety and well-being of occupants inside. The Supreme Court also addressed the reasonableness of a search conducted by a police department targeting an officer's department-issued pager, the constitutionality of a civil commitment statute allowing for the continued commitment of federal inmates determined to be sexually dangerous, and whether the Second Amendment applies to states.

This article provides a brief synopsis of these cases. As always, law enforcement agencies must ensure that their own state laws and constitutions have not provided greater protections than the U.S. constitutional standards.

## DECIDED CASES

*BERGHUIS V. THOMPKINS*, 130 S. CT. 2250 (2010)
In this case, the Supreme Court addressed the impact that silence has on attempts to interrogate an in-custody subject and whether officers could proceed with a custodial interview in the absence of an explicit waiver of *Miranda* rights. The subject in this case was arrested for his involvement in a murder, and detectives, after advising him of his *Miranda* rights, attempted to interrogate him. The subject largely remained silent; then, about 2 hours and 45 minutes into the interrogation, a detective asked if he believed in God, which the subject indicated he did. The detective then asked, "Do you pray for God to forgive you for shooting down that boy?" The subject responded, "yes."[2] Authorities sought to use this admission against him. The lower courts allowed the statement to be used, but the Sixth Circuit Court of Appeals ruled in favor of the defendant.[3] The Supreme Court reversed this decision and found no *Miranda* violation.[4]

The Supreme Court explained that the subject's mere silence in the face of questioning was not a clear and unambiguous invocation of his right to remain silent. Previously, the Court had ruled that to effectively invoke the *Miranda* right to counsel, a subject must do so clearly and unambiguously.[5] In Berghuis, the Court acknowledged that there was no reason to apply different standards, depending on whether the subject invokes the *Miranda* right to counsel or right to silence. Accordingly, the invocation of either the right to silence or the right to counsel must be clear and unambiguous to be effective.

The Supreme Court also considered the defendant's claim that his statement still should be suppressed because he never adequately waived his right to silence. At first blush, this argument appears to have merit in light of the language in the original *Miranda* opinion emphasizing the heavy burden imposed on the government to demonstrate that a valid waiver was obtained and that "a valid waiver will not be presumed simply from the silence of the accused after warnings are given or simply from the fact that a confession was in fact eventually obtained."[6]

However, the Supreme Court has clarified its position in post-*Miranda* cases, emphasizing that *Miranda* is designed to ensure that the subject is advised of and understands certain rights and that, if invoked, these rights are safeguarded.[7] In Berghuis, the Court held that "Where the prosecution shows that a *Miranda* warning was given and that it was understood by the accused, an accused's uncoerced statement establishes an implied waiver of the right to remain silent."[8] By responding to the detective's question, the suspect demonstrated a willingness to waive his right to silence.

The Supreme Court also rejected the defendant's argument that even if he provided a valid waiver, the detectives were not permitted to question him until they obtained the waiver first. The Court noted that there are practical reasons why a waiver should not be required for an interrogation to begin as the interrogation can provide the subject with additional information to help the subject decide whether to invoke or to talk with law enforcement. As stated by the Court, "As questioning commences and then continues, the suspect has the opportunity to consider the choices he or she faces and to make a more informed decision, either to insist on silence or to cooperate."[9] *Miranda* is satisfied "if a suspect receives adequate *Miranda* warnings, understands them, and has an opportunity to invoke the rights before giving any answers or admissions."[10]Accordingly, "after giving a *Miranda* warning, police may interrogate a suspect who has neither invoked nor waived his or her *Miranda* rights."[11]

### MARYLAND V. SHATZER, 130 S. CT. 1213 (2010)

In *Maryland v. Shatzer*, the Court ruled on the legal significance and definition of a break in custody within the context of the Fifth Amendment privilege against self-incrimination.[12] Post-*Miranda* cases expanded on the protections afforded an in-custody subject. In Edwards v. Arizona, [13] the Supreme Court ruled that once defendants invoke their *Miranda* right to counsel, any interrogation must cease, and there can be no further police-initiated interrogation without the presence of counsel. *Edwards* creates a presumption that once in-custody subjects invoke their right to counsel, any subsequent waiver of *Miranda* rights prompted by police-initiated interrogation is itself the result of improper police coercion and, thus, not voluntary.[14]

The *Maryland v. Shatzer* case presented an opportunity to clarify at what point the *Miranda*-Edwards protection would be lifted, permitting police-initiated interrogation following an invocation of the *Miranda* right to counsel.

In *Shatzer*, the defendant was serving a sentence stemming from a child sexual abuse prosecution. A detective attempted to interview the incarcerated subject regarding allegations that he sexually abused his 3-year-old son. Shatzer initially waived his rights, believing that the detective was there to talk with him about why he was in prison, but, upon realizing the detective was there to talk about the new allegation, Shatzer declined to speak without his attorney present. Shatzer was returned to the general prison population. Nearly 2 ½ years later and after developing new evidence, another detective went to the prison to talk with Shatzer about the allegations that he molested his son. The detective advised him of his *Miranda* rights, and, this time, Shatzer waived his rights in writing. Subsequently, Shatzer made incriminating statements. He later was charged with various sexual abuse charges and sought to have the statements he provided suppressed.

Shatzer argued that because he remained in continuous custody following his invocation of his *Miranda* right to counsel, law enforcement could not initiate any contact with him while he remained in custody and that any waiver of his *Miranda* rights provided at the request of law enforcement was not valid. The trial court disagreed with Shatzer's assertion, concluding that given the passage of time, a sufficient break in custody occurred, permitting detectives to reinitiate contact with Shatzer despite his continued incarceration.[15]

The Maryland Court of Appeals reversed the trial court's ruling, holding that the passage of time alone will not suffice to create a break in custody for purpose of the *Miranda*-Edwards rule.[16] The Supreme Court agreed to hear the case to clarify what will constitute a sufficient break in custody and the impact of incarceration on the *Miranda*-Edwards protection.

The Supreme Court ruled that a break in custody alone will not end the *Miranda*-Edwards protection. The Court instead called for a "cooling off" period, prohibiting law enforcement from attempting to interview a subject who previously invoked his *Miranda* right to counsel for 14 days from his release from custody. According to the Court, 14 days gives "plenty of time for the suspect to get reacliminated to his normal life, consult with friends and counsel, and shake off any residual coercive effects of prior custody."[17]

Applying this principle to Shatzer who was incarcerated, as opposed to pretrial detention, the traditional freedom-of-movement test does not resolve the issue of custody. The Court distinguished between incarceration in the general prison population and pretrial detention and found that there was a sufficient break in custody (over 14 days) following Shatzer's initial interrogation until the detective reinitiated contact with him.18 Thus, the waiver obtained from Shatzer was not the product of coercion, and his statements were admissible.

### FLORIDA V. POWELL, 130 S. CT. 1195 (2010)

In this case, the Supreme Court addressed the adequacy of *Miranda* warnings contained within standard advice-of-rights forms used by the Tampa, Florida, Police Department (TPD). The defendant alleged that the form insufficiently advised him of his right to have counsel present during an interrogation. In *Miranda*, the Supreme Court held that prior to custodial interrogation, a defendant must be advised that he has, among other rights, "the right to consult with a lawyer and to have the lawyer with him during interrogation."[19] The TPD form did not expressly state this, but, rather, advised the defendant of his right to talk with an attorney before answering any questions and that he could invoke this right "at any time...during the interview."[20]

The Florida Supreme Court concluded that the form did not satisfy the mandate of *Miranda*.[21] The U.S. Supreme Court reversed, holding that the form communicated the essential message of *Miranda* despite the lack of adherence to its precise language. The Supreme Court again refused to require rigid compliance to precise language, instead focusing on whether, taken as a whole, the language adequately communicated to the defendant that he had the opportunity to consult with counsel during the interview.[22] The defendant was advised of his right to consult with counsel before answering any questions and that he could invoke this right during the interrogation. The Supreme Court stated, "in combination, the two warnings reasonably conveyed [the] right to have an attorney present, not only at the outset of interrogation, but at all times."[23]

### *MICHIGAN V. FISHER*, 130 S. CT. 546 (2009)

Police officers responded to a disturbance call, and, as they approached the area, a couple directed them to a residence where they said a man was "going crazy." The officers continued to the home and found property damaged, as well as drops of blood on the hood of a pickup truck parked in front, clothes sitting inside of it, and one of the doors leading into the house. Through a window, they could see Jeremy Fisher inside the house, yelling and throwing objects.

The officers knocked on the door, but Fisher refused to answer. He also ignored their inquiries as to whether he needed medical attention and directed them to get a search warrant. One of the officers then pushed the front door partially open and saw Fisher pointing a gun in his direction. Eventually, the officers gained control over Fisher and secured the premises.

Fisher was charged with assault with a dangerous weapon and possessing a weapon during the commission of a felony.[24] The trial court granted Fisher's motion to suppress the gun, agreeing with him that it was seized in violation of his Fourth Amendment rights. This was upheld by the Michigan Court of Appeals after it concluded that the warrantless entry violated Fisher's Fourth Amendment rights as the situation "did not rise to the level of an emergency justifying the warrantless intrusion into a residence."[25] The court continued by noting that while there was some indication of a possible injury, "the mere drops of blood did not signal a likely serious, life-threatening injury."[26] The Michigan Supreme Court agreed to hear the case, but, after hearing oral arguments, vacated its order and let the lower court ruling stand.

The Supreme Court reversed, concluding that the state courts rulings were inconsistent with its long line of cases interpreting the Fourth Amendment in the context of exigent circumstances, particularly the Court's recent ruling in Brigham City v. Stuart.[27] In Brigham City, the Supreme Court recognized the need for law enforcement to make warrantless intrusions into a person's home "to render emergency assistance to an injured occupant or to protect an occupant from imminent injury."[28] In considering the reasonableness of the entry, the officer's subjective motivation behind the entry—what did the officer really want to look for— and the seriousness of the crime for which they were originally investigating are not relevant. The relevant consideration is whether the officer has an "objectively reasonable basis for believing that a person is in need of aid."[29]

Applying this standard to the facts of the case, the Court found ample support for application of the emergency aid exception, stating, "Officers do not need ironclad proof of a likely serious, life-threatening injury to invoke the emergency aid exception."[30] The Court concluded by stating:

> It does not meet the needs of law enforcement or the demands of public safety to require officers to walk away from a situation like the one they encountered here. Only when an apparent threat has become an actual harm can officers rule out innocuous explanations for ominous circumstances. But '[t]he role of a peace officer includes preventing violence and restoring order, not simply rendering aid to casualties.'[31]

### CITY OF ONTARIO V. QUON, 130 S. CT. 2619 (2010)

A police officer sued his agency and the city he worked for on the grounds that the department's review of text messages sent to and from his department-issued pager violated his Fourth Amendment rights. The Ninth Circuit Court of Appeals concluded that the officer maintained an expectation of privacy in the contents of the pager and that the review of the messages constituted an unreasonable search.[32] The Supreme Court agreed to hear the case.

The pager at issue was provided to the officer by the department to facilitate communication among SWAT team members. The agency had a "Computer Usage, Internet and E-Mail Policy" that did not specifically include pagers, but the department made it clear to employees that it would treat text messages the same as e-mails.[33] The department's contract with the service provider covered a specific number of characters. For several billing cycles, the officer exceeded his allotted character limit. His supervisor informed him that while he could review the messages, he would refrain from doing as long as the officer paid for the excess charges. After several months of exceeding the character limit, management decided to review the messages to determine the necessity of a contract modification. The service provider supplied transcripts of the messages, which, with respect to Officer Quon, were found to contain numerous nonwork-related, inappropriate messages.[34]

The Supreme Court refrained from addressing the issue of whether the officer had an expectation of privacy in the messages sent to and from the pager. The Court noted that the department made it clear that the pager was considered within the scope of the computer use policy. However, it recognized that whether an expectation of privacy existed was uncertain given the impact of statements by the officer's supervisor that he did not intend to review the pager's messages as long as the officer paid the overage. The Supreme Court stated:

> Prudence counsels caution before the facts in the instant case are used to establish far-reaching premises that define the existence, and extent, of privacy expectations enjoyed by employees when using employer-provided communication devices.[35]

The Supreme Court instead based its holding on the reasonableness of the search, assuming there was an expectation of privacy in the contents of the pager. Applying the long-standing workplace search principles set forth in *O'Connor v. Ortega*,[36] the Court concluded that the review of the text messages was reasonable in light of the work-related, noninvestigatory purpose—to determine the adequacy of the contract with the service provider—and that it was conducted in a reasonable manner. The Court saw the review of the transcripts as "an efficient and expedient way to determine whether Quon's overages were the result of work-related messaging or personal use" and not overly intrusive.[37]

### *UNITED STATES v. COMSTOCK*, 130 S. Ct. 1949 (2010)

Federal inmates challenged the constitutionality of a federal civil-commitment statute authorizing the U.S. government to detain a federal inmate certified as sexually dangerous beyond the time the individual otherwise would be released. The Supreme Court concluded that the statute is consistent with Congress' authority to enact laws that are "necessary and proper" for carrying out the powers vested to the federal government by the Constitution.

The statute at issue passed as part of the Adam Walsh Child Protection and Safety Act and codified at Title 18, U.S. Code, section 4248 and allows a federal district court to order at the government's request the civil commitment of an inmate determined to be sexually dangerous.[38] The inmate is afforded a hearing in which the government must support the claim by presenting clear and convincing evidence.

Inmates targeted by this statute challenged its constitutionality on a number of grounds, including that it amounted to a criminal, not civil, action, thus violating the Double Jeopardy Clause, and contained an insufficient legal standard asserting this type of action required proof beyond a reasonable doubt. In addition, they asserted that it exceeded Congress' authority under the Commerce Clause.[39] The district court agreed with the challengers' contentions.[40] On appeal, the Fourth Circuit Court of Appeals declined to address the standard-of-proof question, instead agreeing that the statute exceeded congressional authority.[41] The government sought Supreme Court review.[42]

The Supreme Court rejected the Commerce Clause challenge to the statute, holding that the Constitution provides Congress with ample authority to enact the civil commitment statute at issue.[43] The Court concluded that consistent with congressional authority under the Commerce Clause, the statute is "rationally related to the implementation of a constitutionally enumerated power."[44]

The Court referenced the inherent authority Congress has with respect to matters relating to the handling of federal prisoners, including decisions pertaining to the provision of mental health care and the need to act to protect the public from the dangers these prisoners may pose, and concluded that the statute in question is rationally related to Congress' authority.[45]

In addition, the Court rejected the argument that the statute violated the Tenth Amendment to the Constitution, which states: "The powers not delegated to the United States by the Constitution, nor prohibited by it to the States, are reserved to the States respectively, or to the people." Finding that the statute is within the scope of congressional authority, this area, thus, is not within those matters "not delegated to the United States." Further, the statute takes into account the interests of the states by requiring coordination with the state in which the prisoner is domiciled or tried and encourages the state to assume custody of the individual.[46]

### *MCDONALD V. CITY OF CHICAGO*, 130 S. CT. 3020 (2010)
In this case, the Supreme Court ruled that the Second Amendment right to keep and bear arms for the purpose of self-defense applies not only to the federal government, as determined by *District of Columbia v. Heller*,[47] but to the states under the Due Process Clause of the Fourteenth Amendment. In reaching this decision, the Court concluded that the right to bear

arms for self-defense is "fundamental to our scheme of ordered liberty" and "deeply rooted" in this nation's history.[48] The Court emphasized that this right is not absolute and that the holding "does not imperil every law regulating firearms."[49]

## CASES FOR NEXT TERM
Several cases of interest to the law enforcement community are already scheduled to be heard by the Supreme Court. These include the five presented here.

*THOMPSON V. CONNICK,* 578 F.3D 293 (5TH CIR. 2009), CERT. GRANTED, *CONNICK V. THOMPSON,* 130 S. CT. 1880 (2010)
In a lawsuit brought against the New Orleans District Attorney's Office, a former criminal defendant sued and was awarded 14 million dollars after a jury determined that the prosecutor's office failed to adequately train the prosecutor in the handling of exculpatory evidence. The Supreme Court will consider whether liability imposed on the D.A.'s office for failing to train the prosecutor in a single case is contrary to the traditional strict culpability standards by the Court in *Canton v. Harris*[50] and *Board of Commissioners of Bryan County v. Brown.*[51]

*PEOPLE v. BRYANT,* 768 N.W.2D 65 (2009), CERT. GRANTED, *MICHIGAN V. BRYANT,* 130 S. CT. 1685 (2010)
The Supreme Court again will address the parameters of the accused's Sixth Amendment right to confront witnesses against him in a case involving statements made by a victim shortly after a shooting. The defendant was prosecuted for shooting the victim, who died shortly after being shot and after telling the police that it was the defendant who shot him. The Michigan Supreme Court held that the statements made by the victim were testimonial in nature within the Supreme Court's rulings in *Crawford v. Washington*[52] and *Davis v. Washington*[53] and, thus, could not be used against

him in his trial given he could not confront the witness against him.

### *STAUB v. PROCTOR HOSPITAL*, 560 F.3D 647 (7TH CIR. 2009), *CERT. GRANTED*, 130 S. CT. 2089 (2010)

This case explores the scope of liability under the Uniform Services Employment and Reemployment Rights Act. The Court will consider whether a supervisor's discriminatory animus against an employee's military service should be imputed to the employer, even if that supervisor is not the ultimate decision maker with respect to the employment action taken against the employee claiming discrimination.

### *THOMPSON v. NORTH AMERICAN STAINLESS LP*, 567 F.3D 804 (6TH CIR. 2009), *CERT. GRANTED*, 130 S. CT. 3542 (2010)

In recent terms, the Supreme Court has taken a number of cases to clarify what constitutes unlawful retaliation within the meaning of Title VII of the Civil Rights Act.[54] For the next term, the Supreme Court has agreed to hear another retaliation case to address who may claim retaliation within the meaning of the statute. The Court will consider whether the Sixth Circuit Court of Appeals was correct in ruling that the statute requires a party claiming retaliation to have actually been engaged in a protected activity within the meaning of the statute. This would require a showing that the person either complained of discrimination or opposed the employer's discriminatory practices. In this case, an employee complained of discrimination, and, three weeks later, her fiancé was fired. The fiancé filed his own action alleging retaliation. The Sixth Circuit Court of Appeals dismissed his suit, finding that he did not engage in a protected activity and rejecting a theory of associational retaliation.

## *SNYDER V. PHELPS*, 580 F.3D 206, CERT. GRANTED, 130 S. CT. 1737 (2010)

This case stems from protest activity by members of the Westboro Baptist Church at the funeral of a soldier killed in combat. This group contends that the deaths of U.S. soldiers are punishment for this country's tolerance of homosexuality and presence of gays in the military. The father sued for the pain the protest activity at his son's funeral caused him. A federal judge awarded the father five million dollars. The Supreme Court will consider whether a private individual is permitted state protection from this type of activity and the scope of the First Amendment protection afforded.

### ENDNOTES

[1] *Miranda v. Arizona*, 384 U.S. 436 (1966). In *Miranda*, the Supreme Court created a set of procedural safeguards that must be provided to a suspect once in custody and prior to engaging in interrogation to protect the Fifth Amendment privilege against compelled self-incrimination.

[2] *Berghuis v. Thompkins*, 130 S. Ct. 2250 (2010).

[3] *Thompkins v. Berghuis*, 547 F.3d 572 (6th Cir. 2008).

[4] For a more thorough discussion of the Berghuis decision see Jonathan L. Rudd, "You Have to Speak Up to Remain Silent: The Supreme Court Revisits the *Miranda* Right to Silence," *FBI Law Enforcement Bulletin*, September 2010, 25-30.

[5] *Davis v. United States*, 512 U.S. 452 (1994).

[6] *Miranda* at 475.

[7] See *Colorado v. Connelly*, 479 U.S. 157 (1986); *North Carolina v. Butler*, 441 U.S. 369 (1979).

[8] Berghuis at 2262.

[9] *Id.* at 2264.

[10] *Id.* at 2263.

[11] *Id.* at 2264

[12] For a more thorough discussion of the Shatzer decision see Kenneth A. Myers, "*Miranda* Update: Fifth Amendment Protection and Break in Custody," FBI Law Enforcement Bulletin, May 2010, 26-32.

13 451 U.S. 477 (1981); *Minnick v. Mississippi*, 498 U.S. 146 (1990).

14 *Arizona v. Roberson*, 486 U.S. 675 (1988).

15 *Maryland v. Shatzer*, 130 S. Ct. 1213, 1218 (2010), referring to the trial court's opinion at No. 21-K-06-37799 (Cir. Ct. Washington City, Md., Sept. 14, 2006).

16 Shatzer v. State, 405 Md. 585, 954 A.2d 1118 (Md. 2008).

17 *Maryland v. Shatzer*, 130 S. Ct. 1213, 1223 (2010).

18 The Supreme Court distinguished between incarceration and pretrial detention, noting that coercive pressure exists in the context of pretrial detention as subjects may be focused on what impact their cooperation has on a pending prosecution. This is in contrast to incarceration where subjects are not influenced by these coercive pressures and when interaction with law enforcement is over they are returned to the general prison population where they live in "their accustomed surroundings and daily routine [where] they regain the degree of control they once had over their lives." Shatzer at 1224.

19 *Miranda* at 471.

20 *Florida v. Powell*, 130 S. Ct. 1195, 1199-1200 (2010).

21 *State v. Powell*, 998 So.2d 531 (2008).

22 See *California v. Prysock*, 453 U.S. 355 (1981); *Duckworth v. Eagan*, 492 U.S. 195 (1989).

23 Powell at 1205.

24 *Michigan v. Fisher*, 130 S. Ct. 546 (2009).

25 Fisher at 548, quoting Docket No. 276439, 2008 WL 786515 at 2 (Mich.App. 2008).

26 *Id* at 549.

27 547 U.S. 398, 126 S. Ct. 1943 (2006).

28 130 S.Ct. at 548, quoting Brigham City v. Stuart, 547 U.S. 398 at 403 (2006).

29 *Id., quoting Brigham City* at 406. *See also Mincey v. Arizona*, 437 U.S. 385 (1978).

30 *Id.* at 549 (internal quotation marks omitted).

31 *Id. at 549, quoting Brigham City at 406.*

32 Quon v. Arch Wireless Operating Co., Inc, 529 F.3d 892 (9th Cir. 2008).

33 See City of Ontario v. Quon, 130 S. Ct. 2619, 2625 (2010).

34 *Id.* at 2627. For example, during the month of August 2002, the officer sent or received 456 messages during work hours, of which 57 were work related.

35 *Id.* at 2629.

36 480 U.S. 709, 107 S. Ct. 1492 (1987).

37 *Id.* at 2631, rejecting the Ninth Circuit Court of Appeal's holding that the department had to choose the least intrusive method to conduct this review to satisfy reasonableness, stating, "Even assuming there were ways that [the department] could have performed the search that would have been less intrusive, it does not follow that the search as conducted was unreasonable." *Id.* at 2632.

38 Adam Walsh Child Protection and Safety Act of 2006, Pub.L. No. 109-248, 120 Stat. 587 (2006).

39 130 S. Ct. 1949, 1955 (2010).

40 *United States v. Comstock*, 507 F.Supp.2d 522 (E.D.NC. 2007).

41 *United States v. Comstock*, 551 F.3d 274 (2009).

42 Subsequently, two other federal circuits considered the legislative authority issue, resolving the issue in favor of the government, thus creating a split of opinion on the issue. *See United States v. Volungus*, 595 F.3d 1 (1st Cir. 2010); *United States v. Tom*, 565 F.3d 497 (8th Cir. 2009).

43 In rejecting the Commerce Clause challenge, the Supreme Court drew upon a long line of judicial interpretation of the powers vested in Congress, stating:

> Nearly 200 years ago, this Court stated that the Federal "Government is acknowledged by all to be one of enumerated powers," which means "[e]very law enacted by Congress must be based on one or more of" those powers. But, at the same time, "a government, entrusted with such" powers "must also be entrusted with ample means for their execution.... Let the end be legitimate, let it be within the scope of the constitution, and all means which are appropriate, which are plainly adapted to that end, which are not prohibited, but consist with the letter and spirit of the constitution are constitutional." *United States v. Comstock*, 130 S. Ct. 1949, 1956, quoting *McCulloch v. Maryland*, 4 Wheat., 316, 405-408, 421 (1819).

44 *Comstock* at 1956.

45 *Id.* at 1958-1961.

[46] 130 S. Ct. 1962. The Supreme Court explicitly declined to address any other constitutional challenges to the statute, instead remanding the case to the lower courts where the challengers may pursue these claims. The Supreme Court previously addressed the constitutionality of a state statute addressing sexual predators and creating a civil-commitment scheme in Kansas v. Hendricks, 521 U.S. 346, 117 S. Ct. 2072 (1997). In this case, the Court rejected constitutional challenges to the civil-commitment provision, holding that it did not create criminal proceedings and that involuntary commitment as provided for in the statute was not punitive, thus allowing for a less-than-reasonable-doubt legal standard. Whether the civil-commitment scheme established by section 4248, largely modeled after the provision challenged in the Hendricks case, survives further judicial scrutiny remains to be seen.

[47] 554 U.S. _, 128 S. Ct. 2783 (2008).

[48] 130 S. Ct. 3036.

[49] *Id.* at 3047. Describing appropriate areas of regulation, the Court in Heller recognized, "prohibitions on the possession of firearms by felons and the mentally ill,...laws forbidding the carrying of firearms in sensitive places such as schools and government buildings, or laws imposing conditions and qualifications on the commercial sale of arms." Heller, at 2816-2817.

[50] 489 U.S. 658 (1978).

[51] 520 U.S. 397, 117 S. Ct. 1382 (1997).

[52] 541 U.S. 36, 124 S. Ct. 1354 (2004).

[53] 547 U.S. 813, 126 S. Ct. 2266 (2006).

[54] *See Crawford v. Metropolitan Government of Nashville and Davidson County,* 129 S. Ct. 846 (2009); *Burlington Northern & Santa Fe Railway Co. v. White,* 126 S. Ct. 2405 (2006).

## DISCUSSION QUESTION

In the case of *Berghuis v. Thompkins*, the U.S. Supreme Court held that an in-custody suspect can waive his right to remain silent without explicitly and verbally doing so. In this case, the suspect never said one way or another whether he waived his rights, but after more than 2 hours of interrogation, he made an incriminating statement. As an officer, what could you do in similar circumstances to maximize the odds that the court would agree that it was a voluntary waiver?

## CRITICAL THINKING EXERCISE

Throughout my career, I made many warrantless entries into homes. Some involved chasing criminal suspects into the homes, others related to the probable destruction of evidence, and there were definitely cases when I believed that someone in the home posed a danger to himself or to others.

Keeping in mind that police officers frequently have to make decisions on the spot, in outline form, describe which factors and circumstances should be considered in regard to emergency or exigent circumstances. Use the case of *Michigan v. Fisher* as a guide.

# Supreme Court Cases
## 2010-2011 Term

By Michael J. Bulzomi, J.D.

November 2011: FBI Law Enforcement Bulletin

**E**ACH YEAR, THE U.S. SUPREME COURT DECIDES CASES that impact the everyday operations and management of law enforcement agencies. The 2010 to 2011 term was no different. It included case decisions covering a variety of constitutional and statutory issues that will affect how departments conduct business.

In this term, the Court decided two Sixth Amendment Confrontation Clause cases and one municipal liability case of interest. It also addressed the protection afforded speech in a case involving a government employee. In the criminal genre, there was a case centering on the emergency exception to the Fourth Amendment search warrant requirement, along with a juvenile case addressing the relevance of age and Miranda warnings.

The Court also addressed the scope of retaliation protection under the Fair Labor Standards Act (FLSA) and in a traditional claim of discrimination in a Title VII case. The Court also decided a bias case involving the Uniformed Services Employment and

Reemployment Rights Act (USERRA). The final case involved alleged government retaliation for an employee's exercise of the First Amendment right to petition grievances against the government.

This article provides brief synopses of these cases. As always, law enforcement agencies must ensure that their own state laws and constitutions have not provided greater protections than those offered by U.S. constitutional standards.

### MICHIGAN V. BRYANT, 131 S. CT. 1143 (2011)

In this case, the U.S. Supreme Court decided that statements made during an ongoing emergency by an unavailable witness are not barred from admission at trial and that their admission does not violate the Sixth Amendment Confrontation Clause.

On April 29, 2001, at approximately 3:30 a.m., Detroit police officers responding to a radio dispatch found a man critically wounded in the parking lot of a gas station. The man, Anthony Covington, was questioned as to what happened, who shot him, and where the shooting had occurred. He responded that he had been shot by respondent Bryant at Bryant's house and that he had driven himself to the gas station. Covington died hours later. His statements were used by the police in Bryant's murder trial where Bryant was convicted of second degree murder. Bryant's conviction was reversed by the Michigan Supreme Court, which held that the Sixth Amendment Confrontation Clause rendered Covington's statement's inadmissible testimonial hearsay.[1]

The case was appealed to the U.S. Supreme Court, which held that testimony by police officers at a murder trial regarding the dying victim's identification of the defendant did not violate the defendant's rights under the Confrontation Clause. Because the primary purpose of the victim's statements was to enable police to respond to an ongoing emergency—a shooting—they were admissible at Bryant's trial.[2]

The Court provided two rules to guide the inquiry as to whether the Confrontation Clause would bar a statement. First, the primary purpose test considers the perspectives of both interrogators and the interrogated. In other words, a witness can answer even questions asked in good faith in a way that makes their primary purpose testimonial.

Second, the test is objective; to determine primary purpose, courts should look at the purpose that reasonable people would have in eliciting or giving the statement, rather than at the actual motives of the parties. If the statement was made to meet an ongoing emergency, its primary purpose usually will be innocent.

Whether the emergency is ongoing even after the crime is completed turns largely on the extent of the continuing public danger—an assessment that could depend on the weapon used in the crime, the likelihood that the assailant will strike again, the medical condition of the victim, and other case-specific circumstances.[3] The Supreme Court determined that the statements at issue were obtained primarily for investigative purposes, and, thus, their use at trial did not violate the Sixth Amendment.

### *BULLCOMING V. NEW MEXICO*, 131 S. CT. 2705 (2011)

The Court decided that the testimony of a lab analyst who had no role in the testing of trial evidence would not satisfy the Sixth Amendment Confrontation Clause requirements. The petitioner, Donald Bullcoming, was arrested for drunk driving. Tests revealed that his blood-alcohol level was three times the legal limit.

Prior to Bullcoming's trial, the lab analyst who had conducted the tests and signed the lab reports had been placed on unpaid leave, so another lab analyst was called to the stand to testify concerning the report. The analyst who testified had neither participated in nor observed the performed tests. The Supreme Court of New Mexico decided that it was not necessary for the lab analyst who conducted the tests to testify as long as a lab analyst testified that the Sixth Amendment Confrontation Clause would be satisfied.[4]

The U.S. Supreme Court disagreed. In 2009, it had decided in Melendez-Diaz v. Massachusetts that a lab report was a form of testimony; as such, the Confrontation Clause required the authors of the report to take the stand for cross-examination.[5] Here, the question was whether another lab analyst could testify in place of the one who actually performed the tests. In a 5 to 4 decision, the Court determined that testimony by a substitute witness does not satisfy the Confrontation Clause. The Court reasoned that given the nature of the examination, a defendant must have an opportunity to dissect the examiner's work by way of confrontation.[6]

### *CONNICK V. THOMPSON*, 131 S. CT. 1350 (2011)

In this case, the Court decided that the district attorney's office should not be held liable under Section 1983 for failure to train its prosecutors based on a single *Brady* violation.[7] Thompson was convicted of murder, sentenced to death, and served 17 years in prison, where he came within a month of his execution date. He had chosen not to testify at his trial because of his fear that the prosecution would bring up an earlier conviction for armed robbery to try to make him look less believable.

However, unbeknownst to Thompson and his attorneys, the prosecutor had blood evidence that would have exonerated him from guilt in the armed robbery case. Had he not been convicted of armed robbery, he could have testified in his own defense in the murder case, and the outcome could have been different. In fact, he was acquitted in a new trial once the blood evidence came to light. After his release from prison, Thompson filed a federal civil rights lawsuit pursuant to Title 42, Section 183, U.S. Code against the district attorney's office, alleging that a Brady violation involving the failure to disclose the exonerating blood evidence was caused by the office's deliberate indifference to an obvious need to train its prosecutors to avoid such constitutional errors.

The U.S. Supreme Court found that although the prosecutors should have given Thompson the blood evidence, when misconduct by prosecutors leads to a wrongful conviction, the agency can be held liable for its employee's actions only if the policy maker for the agency was aware of a pattern of similar bad behavior in the office, yet still did not start a training program for prosecutors.

In *City of Canton, Ohio v. Harris*, the Court noted that it had, in fact, left open the possibility that the unconstitutional consequences of a single incidence of failure to train could be so patently obvious that a city could be held liable under Section 1983 without proof of a preexisting pattern of violations.[8] However, the Court noted that this was not such a case as lawyers are equipped with the tools to seek out, interpret, and apply legal principals prior to obtaining their positions with the government, so additional training would not necessarily be required for them to do their jobs within the confines of the Constitution.[9] Thus, a single Brady violation would not constitute deliberate indifference; a pattern of similar violations would be necessary to establish that a "policy of inaction" constituted the functional equivalent of a decision by the city itself to violate the Constitution.

### *SNYDER V. PHELPS*, 131 S. CT. 1207 (2011)

According to the U.S. Supreme Court, political picketing at a military funeral, even if offensive in its content and manner, is constitutionally protected if it addresses matters of public concern. Fred Phelps, the founder of the Westboro Baptist Church in Topeka, Kansas, and six of his followers picketed the funeral of Marine Lance Corporal Mathew Snyder, an Iraq War veteran. The protest centered on their belief that God hates the United States for its tolerance of homosexuality. The protestors verbally conveyed their message of intolerance and used signs with messages, such as "Thank God for Dead Soldiers" and "America is Doomed." The protest was regarded as peaceful and occurred on public property approximately 1000 feet from the church holding the service.

Snyder's father sued Phelps and his church under state tort law, alleging intentional infliction of emotional distress and invasion of privacy. A jury found Phelps and his church liable for millions of dollars in compensatory and punitive damages.

Phelps appealed, arguing that the First Amendment is violated when a state law allows for infringement on First Amendment protected speech. The Fourth Circuit Court of Appeals reversed the jury determination, granting First Amendment protection for the speech because it centered on matters of public concern, was not provably false, and consisted of participants expressing it solely through hyperbolic rhetoric.[10]

The case also was appealed to the U.S. Supreme Court, which recognized that the contours of what constitutes protected speech is not well defined. However, speech still is protected despite its repugnant nature when it addresses a matter of public concern. The Court has determined that speech relating to matters of political, social, or general interest, value, or concern to the community generally is a matter of public concern. The Court advised that an examination of a statement's content, form, and context decides a matter of public concern, not its inappropriate or controversial character.

The Court decided that the content of the speech in this case related to public matters, such as the moral conduct of the United States and its citizens, not private concerns. The context was on social issues and did not involve personal attacks upon Snyder. The speech occurred on public property in a peaceful manner and did not disrupt the funeral. The Court stated that even hurtful speech on public matters is protected to ensure that public debate is not stifled.[11]

### *KENTUCKY V. KING*, 131 S. Ct. 1849 (2011)

The Court determined that an exigent circumstance created by the arrival of law enforcement officers at a residence does not negate the emergency warrant exception. A search of an apartment in Lexington, Kentucky, took place after the controlled purchase of crack cocaine outside the complex. The suspect dealer walked into the apartment breezeway and entered a residence. The pursuing police officers did not receive the radio call with the information as to which apartment the suspect entered.

The officers stood between two apartments, not knowing which one the suspect had entered, smelled burning marijuana, knocked on the suspect's apartment door, and announced their presence. The residents of the apartment did not respond, but the officers heard noises indicating that the occupants were in the process of destroying the drug evidence. The police officers announced their intentions to enter;

made a warrantless, forced entry; and found three individuals smoking marijuana, as well as, in plain view, cocaine. The officers subsequently found crack cocaine, cash, and drug paraphernalia. The original drug suspect later was apprehended in another apartment.

The respondent, Mr. King, one of the three occupants of the first apartment, was convicted of distribution charges and sentenced to 11 years imprisonment. He appealed his conviction. The Kentucky Court of Appeals affirmed his conviction, stating that the entry into the home was justified under the emergency search warrant exception because the police reasonably believed that the drug evidence would be destroyed and that they did not impermissibly create the exigency because they had not deliberately evaded the warrant requirement.

The Supreme Court of Kentucky reversed, stating that the police could not rely on the exigent circumstances exception if it was reasonably foreseeable that the investigative technique used would result in the exigent circumstances.[12] Hence, knocking and announcing inevitably would induce the destruction of the evidence.

The U.S. Supreme Court assumed that exigent circumstances existed in this case, meaning there was a reasonable belief that evidence would be destroyed unless entry was made. Because exigent circumstances existed, the only question was whether the actions of the police were allowable. The Court decided that as the officers had not violated or threatened to violate the Fourth Amendment prior to the exigency, the warrantless entry was justified.[13] The likelihood that the police notifying suspects of their presence will result in the individuals destroying the evidence, thus creating exigency, has no bearing on the validity of a warrantless entry.

### *J.D.B. v. North Carolina*, 131 S. Ct. 2394 (2011)

In this case, the Supreme Court advised that age is a factor when deciding whether to provide the Miranda advice of rights to a juvenile suspect, but clarified that age is not a determining factor. J.D.B., a 13 year old, was pulled out of class and taken to a conference room at his school, where school administrators and a uniformed police officer questioned him about some items stolen from neighborhood homes. J.D.B. eventually confessed to stealing the items.

His attorney later argued that his confession could not be used because he had not received Miranda warnings. The North Carolina Supreme Court rejected that argument.[14] J.D.B. then filed a petition for certiorari in which he argued that because he was a minor, he would not reasonably believe that he was free to leave when confronted by a police officer and, therefore, must receive Miranda warnings prior to being interrogated.

The U.S. Supreme Court reversed the North Carolina Supreme Court. In a 5 to 4 opinion authored by Justice Sotomayor, the Court held that a minor's age can be a relevant factor when determining whether he or she is in custody. The Court reasoned that while the determination of custody is still an objective one, including consideration of a minor's age in that objective determination is appropriate given the psychological differences between adults and juveniles. This is not to say that age is the decisive factor, but it recognizes that age is to be considered given that a reasonable adult may view the circumstances differently than a reasonable juvenile.[15] The case was remanded back to the North Carolina Supreme Court to determine whether the factoring of age into the analysis occurred while J.D.B. was in custody.

## KASTEN V. SAINT GOBAIN PERFORMANCE PLASTICS CORP., 131 S. CT. 1325 (2011)

The FLSA contains an antiretaliation provision protecting employees who complain of unfair labor practices. However, some question arose as to what kind of complaint qualifies for protection under the act. The FLSA refers to filing a complaint. The act does not specify how this must be done, leaving the Court to determine whether a written complaint is necessary or if an oral complaint satisfies the FLSA. The Court held that a complaint could be filed orally.

Kevin Kasten alleged unlawful retaliation from his employer, Saint Gobain Performance Plastics Corp., which fired him for orally complaining to company officials concerning the location of time clocks, which prevented workers from claiming donning and doffing time for protective gear required for work. The company claimed that it dismissed Kasten after repeated warnings for failing to properly record his comings and goings on the time clock. The district court granted summary judgment in favor of the employer, holding that the act did not allow protection for oral complaints. The Seventh Circuit Court of Appeals affirmed the district court's decision.[16]

The U.S. Supreme Court granted certiorari, holding that an oral complaint is protected under the FLSA antiretaliation provision. The Court used several different tools of statutory interpretation to reach that result. It pointed out that the dictionary definitions of the word *filed* varied, but that the purpose of the act— to protect employees with legitimate complaints— would be undermined if the act required all complaints to be in writing.[17] The Court also noted that many state legal systems allow for oral filings and that the agency charged with administering the FLSA regarded oral complaints as falling under the act. The Court concluded that the Seventh Circuit Court of Appeals erred in determining that oral complaints do not fall within the scope of the act's antiretaliation provision and left the question of whether Kasten could meet the act's notice requirement for the lower courts to decide. The case was vacated and remanded to the Seventh Circuit Court of Appeals. This ruling lessened the need for a high degree of formality when seeking protection from retaliation based on conduct protected by the FLSA.

### *STAUB V. PROCTOR HOSPITAL*, 131 S. CT. 1186 (2011)

An employer can be liable for discrimination under the USERRA if a decision detrimental to an employee is influenced by bias, even if the person who actually makes the detrimental decision is not the biased party. Staub was fired after his two immediate supervisors, who were hostile to him in regard to his military reserve status, mandated additional reporting requirements for him, which they later claimed he did not do. This failure to follow the requirements was forwarded to his supervisor's superior who made the decision to fire Staub. In turn, Staub filed a grievance claiming the underlying reason for his disciplinary warning was that his supervisors were hostile toward his military obligations as a U.S. military reservist. Staub cited a history of work-scheduling conflicts requiring him to take leave or work additional shifts to fulfill his reservist obligations, as well as numerous derogatory comments concerning the military and his duties as a reservist.

This claim was brought under a "cat's paw" theory alleging that Proctor Hospital was liable for the animus of Staub's supervisors who did not make the actual decision to fire him, but did induce the decision maker to fire him based on the animosity they had towards Staub and his reservist status.[18]

A jury found in favor of Staub and awarded him

$57,740 in damages. On appeal, the Seventh Circuit determined that the cat's paw theory applies only to impute the animosity of a nondecision maker with "singular influence" over a decision maker and remanded to enter judgment in favor of Proctor Hospital.[19]

The U.S. Supreme Court granted certiorari and rejected the circuit court's reasoning. It examined the question of under what circumstances an employer is liable for the unlawful intent of supervisors who cause or influence yet do not make the ultimate employment decision.

In so doing, the Court considered both tort and agency law while focusing on the statutory term "motivating factor in the employer's action" found in the USERRA. Principles of tort law instruct that for intentional torts it is the intended consequences of an act, not simply the act, that determines the state of mind required for liability. Further, principles of agency law provide that both the supervisor and the ultimate decision maker, if both acting within the scope of their employment, are agents of the employer, and, thus, their wrongful conduct may be imputed to the employer.

The Court concluded that the evidence suggested that a reasonable jury could have inferred that the actions of the supervisor were motivated by hostility toward Staub's military obligations and that these actions were causal factors underlying the ultimate decision to fire Staub.[20] The Court reversed the Seventh Circuit opinion and remanded for further proceedings to determine whether a new trial was warranted. This decision has the potential to affect liability issues in other federal acts, such as Title VII and the American with Disabilities Act (ADA), which has language similar to the USERRA.

## THOMPSON V. NORTH AMERICAN STAINLESS, 131 S. CT. 863 (2011)

This case continued the Supreme Court's broad interpretation of the antiretaliation provision within federal antidiscrimination law.[21] Eric Thompson, an engineer at North American Stainless, a stainless steel manufacturer, was fired after his then-fiancée (now wife) filed a gender-discrimination complaint with the Equal Employment Opportunity Commission (EEOC). Thompson argued that because the company could not legally fire his fiancée in retaliation for her complaint, it fired him instead. At question in the case is whether Title VII—a federal antidiscrimination law—protects close family members and friends of a complaining employee or only the employee from retaliatory employer action.

The U.S. District Court for the Eastern District of Kentucky granted summary judgment to North American Stainless, finding that Title VII does not permit third-party retaliation claims. The Sixth Circuit Court of Appeals met en banc after a panel of the Sixth Circuit reversed the district court decision and affirmed the district court ruling.[22]

The case then was appealed to the U.S. Supreme Court, which advised that Title VII protects any employee who has made a charge under the act from employer discrimination.[23] Title VII also allows any person claiming to be aggrieved by an unlawful employment practice to file charges with the EEOC or even sue the employer if the EEOC declines to do so.[24]

The Court then looked to the two issues presented by this case: First, if Thompson's firing by his employer was unlawful retaliation and, second, if so, if Thompson was entitled to relief under Title VII. The Court stated that if Thompson's statement of fact was true, then he was the subject of unlawful retaliation.[25] The Court went on to say that Thompson was covered under Title VII due to the retaliation provision, which prohibits any employer action that "well might have dissuaded a reasonable worker from making or supporting a discrimination charge."[26] In regard to the issue of the proverbial "slippery slope" as to where protection against retaliation begins and ends and who is covered, the Court stated that no general rule should be made as any such rule would restrict the number of claimants unduly but that common sense should prevail because "the significance of any given act of retaliation will depend upon the particular circumstances."[27]

### *BOROUGH OF DURYEA, PENNSYLVANIA V. GUARNIERI*, 131 S. CT. 2488 (2011)

Embedded within the First Amendment is an individual's right to "petition the Government for a redress of grievances."[28] The parameters of this right were tested with the result being similar to what is seen in speech cases involving government employees.

Police Chief Charles J. Guarnieri was fired by the Borough of Duryea, Pennsylvania, in 2003 and subsequently filed a grievance to fight the firing. After arbitration, Chief Guarnieri was reinstated. Upon returning to his job, he found that the council had issued a number of directives limiting the tasks he could and could not do as chief. He then filed a second grievance, which resulted in the modification of the directives.

He also sued the borough, alleging retaliation over his having filed the first grievance in 2003. Chief Guarnieri did so on the basis that the retaliation was a violation of his First Amendment right to petition. A jury found for Chief Guarnieri, and the borough appealed to the U.S. Third Circuit Court of Appeals, citing that only matters of public concern were protected under the First Amendment. The Third Circuit held that the First Amendment right to petition protects public employees concerning any manner, public or personal.[29]

The U.S. Supreme Court granted certiorari to determine the limitations of retaliation protection under the First Amendment right to petition. The Court long has held that for speech by a government employee to be protected under the First Amendment, it must address a matter of public concern.[30]

Even if it addresses a matter of public concern before it is afforded protection, the Court must undergo a balancing-of-interests test between the government's need to manage its internal affairs and the interests of the individual in expressing matters of public concern to determine if the speech truly is protected. In this case involving the right to petition, the Court reasoned that a similar rubric should apply.

The Court determined that to do otherwise in petition cases would undermine government efficiency and cause undue lawsuits in federal courts dealing with internal management issues better left to internal resolution procedures, the states, or appropriate federal statutes that deal with employment issues.[31]

The Court decided that a public employee's right to petition is a right to participate as a citizen in the democratic process, but not a right to transform everyday employment disputes into constitutional issues for federal litigation. For a public employee to bring a case involving the right to petition, there must be a matter of public concern.

## Cases of Interest in the 2011-2012 Term

The U.S. Supreme Court has placed a number of cases of interest to law enforcement agencies on next year's docket. One of particular interest is United States v. Jones, where the court will decide whether the warrantless prolonged use of a global positioning system (GPS) tracking device to monitor a vehicle's movement on public streets violates the Fourth Amendment protection against unreasonable searches and seizures.[32]

The second case of interest is Messerschmitt v. Millender, where the court will consider whether police officers are entitled to qualified immunity where they execute search warrants later deemed invalid.[33] In Florence v. Board of Freeholders, the Court has been asked to determine whether the Fourth Amendment permits strip searches by jailors for all offenses, including minor ones, without acting out of suspicion.[34]

The final case of interest is Howes v. Fields, which involves Miranda and prison inmates.[35] The Court will determine whether a prisoner always is considered in custody for purposes of Miranda when the prisoner is isolated from the general prison population and questioned concerning conduct occurring outside the facility.

ENDNOTES

[1] 768 N.W.2d 65 (Mich. 2009).
[2] 131 S. Ct. 1143, at 1168.
[3] Id. at 1150.
[4] 226 P.3d 1 (N.M. 2010).
[5] 129 S. Ct. 2527 (2009).
[6] 131 S. Ct. 2705, at 2716.
[7] *Brady v. Maryland,* 88 S. Ct. 1194 (1963).
[8] 109 S. Ct. 1197 (1989).
[9] 131 S. Ct. 1350, at 1361.
[10] 131 S. Ct. 1207, at 1210.
[11] *Id.* at 1220.
[12] 302 S.W.3d 649 (2010).
[13] *Id.* at 1863.
[14] 686 S.E.2d 135 (2009).

[15] 131 S. Ct. 2394, at 2404.

[16] 570 F.3d 834 (2009).

[17] 131 S. Ct. 1325, at 1331.

[18] "Cat's paw" comes from Jean de la Fontaine's *The Monkey and the Cat*, a fable involving a devious monkey who persuades an unsuspecting cat to take chestnuts from a fire. The cat burns its paws, while the monkey eats the chestnuts unscathed. Although it was the cat that was burned, the monkey induced the cat to take such action, making the cat an agent of the monkey's devious purpose. The cat's paw theory applied in the context of employment discrimination imputes liability to an employer for an adverse employment action taken by a nondiscriminating decision maker (the cat) induced into taking such action by the discrimination of another employee (the monkey).

[19] 560 F.3d 647 (2009).

[20] 131 S. Ct. 1186, at 1194.

[21] See also *Crawford v. Metropolitan Government of Nashville and Davidson County*, 129 S. Ct. 846 (2009); and *Burlington Northern and Santa Fe Railway* Co. v. White, 126 S. Ct. 2405 (2006).

[22] 567 F.3d 804 (2009).

[23] Title 42 U.S.C. § 2000e-3(a).

[24] *Id.* at 2000e-5(b), (f)(1).

[25] 131 S. Ct. 863, at 866.

[26] Id. at 869.

[27] See *Burlington N. & S.F.R. Comp. v. White*, 548 U.S. 59, at 69.

[28] First Amendment of the U.S. Constitution.

[29] 364 Fed. Appx. 749 (C.A.3 2010).

[30] See *Connick v. Myers*, 461 U.S. 138 (1983); and City of San Diego v. Roe, 125 S. Ct. 521 (2004).

[31] 131 S. Ct. 2488, at 2497.

[32] *U.S. v. Maynard*, 615 F.3d 544 (2010).

[33] *Millender v. County of Los Angeles*, 620 F.3d 1016 (2010).

[34] *Florence v. Board of Chosen Freeholders of County of Burlington*, 621 F.3d 296 (2010).

[35] *Fields v. Howes*, 617 F.3d 813 (2010).

---

*Law enforcement officers of other than federal jurisdiction who are interested in this article should consult their legal advisors. Some police procedures ruled permissible under federal constitutional law are of questionable legality under state law or are not permitted at all.*

---

### DISCUSSION QUESTION

Which of the cases discussed in this article had the most impact on our criminal justice system? You can discuss this from the perspective of a suspect, a victim, or the prosecution, or any combination thereof.

## CRITICAL THINKING EXERCISE

As an investigator, I always bore in mind that there are numerous exceptions to the hearsay rule. In doing so, I endeavored to build complex criminal cases by preparing to use these statements at trial. The Supreme Court, in the case of *Michigan v. Bryant,* supports this position.

As a team, list in outline form as many exceptions to the hearsay rule that you believe could enhance a criminal prosecution. In the process, make sure you make note of how you might strengthen the utility of the exception and ultimately the admissibility of the statement.

You should also have a good understanding of the concept of an out-of-court-statement not "going to the truth of the matter asserted."

# SUPREME COURT CASES
## 2011-2012 TERM

By Kevin Chechak, J.D.

November 2012: FBI *Law Enforcement Bulletin*

**D**URING THE CURRENT TERM, THE SUPREME COURT decided cases of importance to law enforcement, including those involving procedure, substantive law, and law enforcement liability. In one case with immediate consequences, the court ruled that attaching a global positioning system (GPS) device on the undercarriage of a car constituted a Fourth Amendment search.

The court elaborated further on the role of *Miranda* in interviews occurring in a prison setting, as well as the government's duty to produce potentially exculpatory evidence under *Brady*. In a civil suit against law enforcement officers, the court addressed the proper role of qualified immunity and whether the law was clearly defined at the time the government acted. Also, the court struck down a substantive criminal statute as being violative of the First Amendment.

This article provides a brief synopsis of each of these cases, as well as a summary of cases of interest to law enforcement that the Supreme Court has agreed to hear in the 2012-2013 term. As always, law enforcement agencies must ensure that their own state laws and constitutions have not provided greater protections than the U.S. constitutional standards.

## DECIDED CASES

*UNITED STATES V. JONES*, 132 S. CT. 945 (2012)

In this case the U.S. Supreme Court revived the doctrine that a physical intrusion by the government into a constitutionally protected area for the purpose of gathering information is a Fourth Amendment search, a principle most courts had considered subsumed by the reasonable expectation of privacy standard. As part of a drug conspiracy investigation, officers obtained a warrant from the U.S. District Court for the District of Columbia to install a tracking device on a vehicle used by Jones but registered to his wife. The tracking device was to be placed on the vehicle within 10 days. Eleven days after the court order was issued, officers placed the GPS device on the vehicle while it was in Maryland.[1]

The device provided officers with 2,000 pages of location data over the next four weeks. Jones' motion to suppress the GPS information was denied; he was convicted and then appealed. The court of appeals reversed the conviction, finding the warrantless use of the GPS device in violation of the Fourth Amendment.[2] The appellate court held that the use of the GPS device was a search where Jones had a reasonable expectation of privacy in his movements over an extended period of time.[3]

The U.S. Supreme Court unanimously agreed that the use of the GPS was a search under the Fourth Amendment, but filed separate opinions with divergent reasons in support of that conclusion. The majority opinion written by Justice Scalia relied on an originalist interpretation finding the vehicle to be an "effect" within the meaning of the Fourth Amendment and the attachment of the GPS device to a vehicle by government agents to gather information to be a trespass and, therefore, a search within the meaning of the Fourth Amendment. "The government physically occupied private property for the purpose of obtaining information. We have no doubt that such a physical intrusion would have been considered a 'search' within the meaning of the Fourth Amendment when it was adopted."[4]

The opinion expresses that the original theory of governmental trespass as a basis for a Fourth Amendment violation had not been replaced by the theory of "reasonable expectation of privacy" developed in *United States v. Katz.*[5] In *Katz* the court found that the government had violated the Fourth Amendment by placing without a warrant a covert microphone on a public phone booth to overhear a suspect's telephone conversation. *Katz* and cases following it expanded the protection of the Fourth Amendment beyond "persons, houses, papers and effects" (as expressly listed in the Fourth Amendment) and held that the amendment protected people and their reasonable expectation of privacy in less concrete matters, like conversations, telephone calls, and e-mails.

Prior to *Jones* several federal circuit court decisions held that people had no reasonable expectation of privacy in the movement of their vehicles on public streets because those actions are readily observable by anyone—including the government—and, therefore, use of a GPS device to monitor a vehicle's movement on public streets did not violate any reasonable expectation of privacy.[6] In each of those cases, the courts held that the act of the physical installation itself of a slap-on or magnetic GPS device on the vehicle did not independently constitute a search under the Fourth Amendment. *Jones* overrules such decisions when placing a tracking device on the vehicle requires a physical touching of the vehicle with the intention of gathering information. The court did not overrule prior decisions where the tracking device already was in place before the subject took possession of the object to be tracked because there was no trespass.[7] In addition, the decision leaves open the question of the constitutionality of electronic tracking, which is feasible by nonphysical means, such as monitoring a subject's movements through GPS signals emitted by a subject's cellular telephone.[8]

Justice Sotomayor joined with the majority opinion in holding that here the physical trespass on a constitutionally protected "effect" (the vehicle) constituted a Fourth Amendment search, but filed a concurring opinion agreeing with Justice Alito's concurrence that long-term GPS monitoring would infringe on an individual's reasonable expectation of privacy. Justice Sotomayor also expressed that in other cases not involving physical intrusion, the *Katz* approach should be applied given concern regarding data aggregation and government accumulation of information. Justice Sotomayor stated, "More fundamentally, it may be necessary to reconsider the premise that an individual has no reasonable expectation of privacy in information voluntarily disclosed to third parties. This approach is ill suited to the digital age, in which people reveal a great deal of information about themselves to third parties in the course of carrying out mundane tasks."[9]

Justice Alito filed a concurrence in the result, joined by three other justices, but believed the case should be decided by applying the *Katz* reasonable expectation of privacy analysis. Alito reasoned that the long-term monitoring of the movement of Jones' vehicle violated his reasonable expectation of privacy. Alito's opinion indicates the reasonable expectation of privacy analysis would encompass all types of surveillance, including old fashioned physical surveillance with cars and aircraft, as well as tracking, which could be achieved remotely as opposed to the need to physically intrude into a protected area. It also indicates the expectation that how long citizens can be followed would differ based on the offense being investigated. While not setting down a matrix of what time limits would be allowable, Justice Alito indicated that 28 days was too long in this drug investigation.

This case was decided based on simple trespass analysis. However, five justices signaled readiness to expand the protections of the Fourth Amendment in future cases to limit government collection and aggregation of publicly available information where such efforts may violate the public's reasonable expectation of privacy.

### *HOWES v. FIELDS,* 132 S. CT. 1181 (2012)

Defendant Fields was serving a sentence in a Michigan jail where he was questioned by sheriff's deputies about alleged child sex abuse unrelated to the crimes for which he was incarcerated. Fields was brought from the general population into a separate section of the facility and put in a conference room with the deputies. The deputies did not read Fields his *Miranda* rights, but did advise him at the beginning and at several other times during the five- to seven-hour interview that he was free to leave at any time and return to his cell. Fields was not handcuffed or restrained, and the door to the room sometimes was open and sometimes closed. At no point did Fields indicate that he wanted to return to his cell. He eventually confessed, and at the conclusion of the interview, he had to wait 20 minutes while a guard was called to return him to his cell.

The Sixth Circuit Court of Appeals applied a categorical rule in concluding that his statements should be suppressed, holding that a prisoner always is in custody for *Miranda* purposes when pulled from the prison population and questioned about criminal conduct.[10]

The Supreme Court rejected this categorical rule, concluding that incarceration in and of itself is not "custody" for purposes of the *Miranda* warnings. *Miranda* custody requires analysis of whether based on the objective circumstances a person would feel free to terminate the interview and leave and whether the limitations on movement present a coercive environment.

The court noted three factors of confinement that normally contribute to a coercive environment, but do not apply to a person serving a jail or prison sentence. An incarcerated individual, as opposed to someone just arrested, is not experiencing any "shock" of custody. In addition, incarcerated individuals (as opposed to those awaiting trial) are unlikely to be lured into speaking by hope for a quick release.

They also know that the questioning officers cannot affect the length of their confinement. Applying these factors to the facts in the present case, the court held that Fields was not in custody for purposes of *Miranda*. As stated by the Supreme Court, "Taking into account all of the circumstances of the questioning—including especially the undisputed fact that respondent was told he was free to end the questioning and return to his cell—we hold that respondent was not in custody within the meaning of *Miranda*."[11]

*SMITH V. CAIN*, 132 S. CT. 627 (2012)

In *Smith* the court ordered a new trial after concluding that the government violated *Brady v. Maryland* by failing to disclose potentially exculpatory material to the defense.[12] In 1992 Larry Boatner was the victim of a home invasion robbery during which five of his friends were killed. Boatner was the only survivor in a position to see the perpetrators. Juan Smith eventually was charged in the crime and prosecuted.

The principle evidence against Smith was testimony by Boatner identifying him as one of the assailants. Notes of the lead detective responding to the scene indicated that Boatner stated shortly after the crime that he could not identify any of the murderers, and his report of a reinterview of Boatner five days later indicated the same. These notes made by the detective were not produced to the defense before trial.

Based on this omission, the court found a *Brady* violation, reiterating that *Brady* established a due process violation where evidence withheld is material to a determination of the defendant's guilt. Evidence is material where there is a reasonable probability that the result of the proceeding would have been different if it was produced. A defendant need only show that the likelihood of a different result is great enough to undermine confidence in the outcome of the trial.[13] Here Boatner testified at trial that he had "no doubt" Smith was the gunman he stood "face to face" with the night of the murders, and Boatner's testimony was the only evidence linking Smith to the crime. The court found Boatner's contradictory statements that he could not identify anyone plainly material.[14]

*MESSERSCHMIDT V. MILLENDER*, 132 S. CT. 1235 (2012)

This case is a civil action under Title 42, Section 1983, U.S. Code for damages against officers, including

Detective Kurt Messerschmidt, alleging violation of Millender's Fourth Amendment rights by an improper search and seizure. Shelly Kelly was moving out from the residence she shared with her boyfriend Jerry Bowen when he attacked her and shot at her with a black sawed-off pistol-grip shotgun as she drove away, striking her car. Detective Messerschmidt researched Bowen, found gang affiliations, and prepared affidavits for a search warrant at the home of Augusta Millender, Bowen's foster mother, where he was believed to be staying.

The warrant sought any and all weapons or ammunition, indicia of gang affiliation, and articles showing who controlled the premises. The warrant was executed while Augusta Millender was home, resulting in the seizure of Millender's shotgun, a social services letter addressed to Bowen, and a box of .45-caliber ammunition. Millender subsequently filed a civil action alleging that the search violated her Fourth Amendment rights.

The officers sought to dismiss the lawsuit on the basis of qualified immunity. The district court and an en banc Ninth Circuit Court of Appeals denied the officers' claim of qualified immunity, concluding that no reasonable officer would have relied on the warrant because it was facially overbroad where it sought all firearms, ammunition and related articles, and a wide variety of gang-related materials where the crime had no relation to gang activity.[15]

The Supreme Court reversed, granting the officers qualified immunity. The court reiterated that officers are entitled to qualified immunity unless their actions violated clearly established statutory or constitutional rights using objective legal reasonableness to evaluate the legal rules established at the time of the conduct. The court agreed with the principle articulated by the Ninth Circuit that while a warrant may be signed by a neutral magistrate, thus establishing a strong indication of objective reasonableness of the officers' behavior, the shield of immunity conferred by the warrant may be lost where the underlying affidavit is so lacking in indicia of probable cause as to render belief in its existence unreasonable.[16] Given the facts and logical inferences that could be drawn in this case, the court concluded that the warrant met the objective reasonableness test.

The court reasoned that an officer could infer that Bowen might have additional weapons and pose a continuing threat with them and that his gang affiliation could bear both on his motive and credibility. Noting the number of supervisors and other officials who reviewed the affidavits, the court stated that the officers were not required to parse through and make a precise probable cause determination by comparing the facts in the affidavit with the items listed in the warrant application.[17]Finding that the warrant application was not so obviously lacking in probable cause such that the officers could be considered plainly incompetent for concluding otherwise, the court ruled they were entitled to qualified immunity.

### *UNITED STATES V. ALVAREZ,* 132 S. CT. 2537 (2012)

Defendant Alvarez had made verbal false statements claiming to be a recipient of the Congressional Medal of Honor. He was charged under Title 18, Section 704, U.S. Code, which makes it a crime to falsely represent verbally or in writing to have been awarded any decoration or medal authorized by Congress for the U.S. Armed Forces. Four justices joined the majority opinion, and two justices joined in a concurring opinion with the plurality decision finding that the statute did not meet the "exacting scrutiny" applied to content-based speech restrictions.[18]

The court held that the statute did not fit within any of the three recognized exceptions to the First Amendment for false statements and distinguished it from cases, such as fraud and defamation, where legally cognizable harm resulted from the falsehood.[19] While all nine justices acknowledged the importance of properly recognizing the heroism and sacrifice of service members, the plurality found that the government did not establish that a new exception to the First Amendment was merited where less restrictive means were available to control the false speech. Effective means to limit the effect of the false speech included counterspeech and resulting public ridicule and establishing a publicly accessible database of actual medal recipients.

## CASES OF INTEREST FOR 2012-2013

*FLORIDA V. HARRIS,* CASE BELOW *HARRIS V. FLORIDA,* 71 SO.3D 756 (FLA. 2011), CERT. GRANTED, 132 S. CT. 1796 (2012)
This case asks what facts, if any, must be presented by the government to establish the reliability of a drug dog's alert beyond the dog's basic training and certification. The Florida Supreme Court held in a case involving the warrantless search of a vehicle after a dog alerted positive to the presence of narcotics to establish probable cause to support a search; relying on the training and certification of the dog *alone* is not sufficient.[20]

*FLORIDA V. JARDINES,* CASE BELOW *JARDINES V. FLORIDA,* 73 SO.3D 34 (FLA. 2011), CERT. GRANTED, 132 S. CT. 995 (2012)
In another Florida drug dog case, the court has agreed to consider whether the use of a drug detection dog at the front door of a premises is a search within the meaning of the Fourth Amendment and if so whether probable cause is required. The Florida Supreme Court decided that it was a search and that an evidentiary showing of wrongdoing establishing probable cause

(not reasonable suspicion) was required before such a search could take place.[21]

**BAILEY V. UNITED STATES, CASE BELOW UNITED STATES V. BAILEY, 652 F.3D 197 (2ND CIR. 2011), CERT. GRANTED, 132 S. CT. 2710 (2012)**

The court will determine whether during the execution of a search warrant targeting premises officers may detain occupants of those premises who have left the location during or immediately before the warrant was executed.

Evidence obtained during the detention was admitted at trial over objections that the detention violated Bailey's Fourth Amendment rights.[22] In *Michigan v. Summers* the Court construed the Fourth Amendment to allow officers executing a search warrant targeting premises to detain an occupant of those premises when they encountered him leaving the location while they were preparing to execute the warrant.[23]

In *Bailey,* officers were preparing to execute a search warrant when they observed Bailey and a friend leave the target residence. Other officers followed them for about a mile, pulled the vehicle over, and detained them. The subjects made incriminating statements during the detention encounter indicating that the search location was Bailey's residence, and keys were taken from Bailey that matched the residence being searched. During the detention, officers at the premises began execution of the search warrant and found a gun and drugs.

Bailey sought to suppress the evidence derived from the detention, claiming it was an unreasonable seizure under the Fourth Amendment and not justified as part of the execution of the search warrant. The Second Circuit Court of Appeals concluded that the detention was reasonable under the Fourth Amendment.[24] The

Supreme Court has agreed to hear this case in light of the conflict that exists at the federal circuit court level.[25]

## VANCE V. BALL STATE UNIVERSITY, CASE BELOW VANCE V. BALL STATE UNIVERSITY, 646 F.3D 461 (7TH CIR. 2011), CERT. GRANTED, __ S. CT. __ (2012)

This is a case of interest to law enforcement managers. The Court will decide whether for purposes of establishing vicarious liability under the *Farragher-Burlington Industries* standard a supervisor is limited to those who have the power to take a final employment action, such as to fire, demote, transfer, or discipline, or can include any person who can direct and oversee the victim's daily work.[26]

## ENDNOTES

[1] As noted by the court at footnote 1, the government conceded noncompliance with the warrant and argued that it did not need a warrant. *United States v. Jones*, 132 S. Ct. 945, 948 (2012).

[2] *United States v. Maynard*, 615 F.3d 544 Cir. (D.C. 2010).

[3] The government did not argue below that if using the GPS was a search that it was, nevertheless, "reasonable" under the Fourth Amendment, and both the appellate and Supreme Court held that this argument had been waived. *See Maynard*, 615 F.3d at 567; and *Jones*, 132 S. Ct. at 954.

[4] *See Jones*, 132 S. Ct. at 949.

[5] *Katz v. United States*, 389 U.S. 347 (1967).

[6] *United States v. Garcia*, 474 F.3d 994 (7th Cir. 2007); *United States v. Pineda-Moreno*, 591 F.3d 1212 (9th Cir. 2010); and *United States v. Marquez*, 605 F.3d 604 (8th Cir. 2010).

[7] *Jones* at 951-952.

[8] For example, in *United States v. Skinner*, No. 09-6497, 2012 WL 3289801 (6th Cir. Aug. 14, 2012), a post-*Jones* case, the defendant was trafficking marijuana from Arizona to Tennessee and using a pay-as-you-go cell phone to coordinate with other co-conspirators. DEA agents identified the defendant's cell phone and "pinged" the phone

to obtain GPS data from it and to locate and arrest the defendant. The court held that there was no Fourth Amendment violation because the defendant had no reasonable expectation of privacy in his publicly visible location traveling on a highway and no expectation of privacy in the information emitting from the phone he chose to use. The court noted that, unlike *Jones,* no device had been attached to the defendant's vehicle.

[9] *See Jones,* 132 S. Ct. at 957.

[10] *Fields v. Howes,* 617 F.3d 813 (6th Cir. 2010).

[11] *Howes v. Fields,* 132 S. Ct. 1181, 1194 (2012).

[12] *Brady v. Maryland,* 373 U.S. 83 (1963).

[13] *Smith v. Cain,* 132 S. Ct. 627, 630 (2012).

[14] *Id.* at 630.

[15] *Millender v. County of Los Angeles,* 620 F.3d 1016 (9th Cir. 2010).

[16] *Messerschmidt v. Millender,* 132 S. Ct. 1235, 1245 (2012).

[17] *Id.* at 1250.

[18] *United States v. Alvarez,* 132 S. Ct. 2537, 2543 (2012).

[19] Those exceptions are prohibition of false statements to a government official, perjury, and falsely claiming to be speaking as a government official or on behalf of the government. *Id.* at 2545-2546; and *Id.* at 2545.

[20] *Harris v. Florida,* 71 So.3d 756 (Fla. 2011).

[21] *Jardines v. Florida,* 73 So.3d 34 (Fla. 2011).

[22] *United States v. Bailey,* 652 F.3d 197 (2nd Cir. 2011).

[23] *Michigan v. Summers,* 452 U.S. 692 (1981).

[24] *See Bailey,* 652 F.3d 197, 206-207.

[25] *See United States v. Cochran,* 939 F.2d 337 (6th Cir. 1991); *United States v. Cavazos,* 288 F.3d 706 (5th Cir. 2002); *United States v. Bullock,* 632 F.3d 1004 (7th Cir. 2011) (extending *Summers* to include occupants detained a short distance from the search location); *United States v. Sherill,* 27 F.3d 344 (8th Cir. 1994); and *United States v. Edwards,* 103 F.3d 90 (10th Cir. 1996) (refusing to extend *Summers* to detentions of occupants away from the search location).

[26] *Farragher v. City of Boca Raton,* 524 U.S. 775 (1998); and *Burlington Industries, Inc. v. Ellerth,* 524 U.S. 742 (1998) [Establishing liability for the harassment caused by supervisors and managers, but permitting employers to assert an affirmative defense demonstrating that they had adequate corrective and preventive policies in place that the

victim-employee failed to take advantage of in cases where the harassment did not lead to a tangible employment action].

*Law enforcement officers of other than federal jurisdiction who are interested in this article should consult their legal advisers. Some police procedures ruled permissible under federal constitutional law are of questionable legality under state law or are not permitted at all.*

---

### DISCUSSION QUESTION

Through the years the courts have held that one factor in determining if a search took place was whether a suspect had a "reasonable expectation of privacy." If not, there could be no violation of the Fourth Amendment. Now the U.S. Supreme Court, in the case of *United States v. Jones,* holds that a "trespass" is sufficient to invoke a Fourth Amendment violation. How to you think this case may or may not affect the "Open Fields" doctrine?

## CRITICAL THINKING EXERCISE

As a group, develop a list of factors or circumstances that might have had a different effect on the admissibly of the statements in the case of *Howes v. Fields* (2012).*
In other words, what the police did here was correct, but the Supreme Court suggests that there could have been police conduct that might have required the Miranda warning.

*132 S. Ct. 1181

# Supreme Court Cases
## 2012 to 2013 Term

By Kevin Chechak, J.D.

January 2014: *FBI Law Enforcement Bulletin*

URING THE 2012 TO 2013 TERM, THE SUPREME COURT decided a number of cases of interest to the law enforcement community, including several involving the Fourth Amendment. These are highlighted by a pair of canine search cases out of Florida, a DUI compelled blood test case, and a case questioning the collection of DNA from arrestees. The Court also decided a case regarding application of the Fifth Amendment in noncustodial interrogations and a vicarious liability case of interest to law enforcement agencies in their roles as employers.

This article provides a brief synopsis of each of these cases and also a summary of cases of interest to law enforcement that the Supreme Court has agreed to hear in the 2013 to 2014 term. As always, law enforcement agencies must ensure that their own state laws and constitutions have not provided greater protections than the U.S. constitutional standards.

# DECIDED CASES

## *FLORIDA V. JARDINES,* 133 S.CT. 1409 (2013)

The question presented in this case was whether a dog sniff at the front door of a suspected grow house by a trained narcotics detection dog was a Fourth Amendment search requiring probable cause. A divided Court held that a search did occur when the officer took his dog onto the front porch of the suspected grow house for the purpose of sniffing for drugs. Justice Scalia, writing for the majority, applied the same reasoning he used in the *United States v. Jones*[1] decision last term, which found a government intrusion into private property for the purpose of gathering information was a trespass and a search under the Fourth Amendment. In *Jones* the trespass in question was the attachment of a GPS tracker to a defendant's automobile.

The trespass issue in the *Jardines* case centered on whether government agents could enter onto the front porch of the home, which, as part of the curtilage of the residence, was entitled to Fourth Amendment protection, in contrast to open fields, which are not protected under the Fourth Amendment.[2]

The government argued the defendant had no reasonable expectation of privacy under *Katz v. United States*[3] in the odors emanating from his home and no reasonable expectation of privacy that police officers or their dogs would not go on his porch to smell those odors.

The Court found an implied license normally exists which allows persons, such as visitors, girl scouts selling cookies, or trick-or-treaters, to approach your door. This kind of implied license also might allow a police officer to approach someone's front door to knock and ask to speak to the individual, but it is not reasonable to think typical people would confer an implied license to allow police to enter upon their curtilage for the purpose of having a drug dog sniff around.[4] The Court further elaborated that people would not expect someone approaching their front door to use a metal detector along the front path or to allow a bloodhound into their garden without first asking permission.[5] As in *Jones,* the majority opinion relied on traditional trespass analysis to reach the conclusion that there was a Fourth Amendment search where the government intruded into a constitutionally protected area to seek information.[6]

### *FLORIDA V. HARRIS,* 133 S.CT. 1050 (2013)

In another drug detection dog related case from Florida, the U.S. Supreme Court reversed the Florida Supreme Court, which had used a strict checklist of evidence to evaluate the reliability of a drug dog's alert as a basis for probable cause to search. This checklist included the dog's training and certification records, evidence concerning the experience and training of the officer handling the dog, and a particular emphasis on field records of the dog's performance, including how many times the dog alerted, but no contraband was subsequently found.[7] The Court held probable cause should be determined based on the totality of the circumstances, not an inflexible checklist.[8]

The defendant also wanted to use field records of the dog's performance and false positives where the dog alerted, but no drugs were found, to challenge the dog's reliability as a basis for probable cause. The Court held that the absence of such records was not fatal to the state's case and, more important, that records of the dog's performance in controlled testing and certification were more probative of the dog's reliability. The court acknowledged that dogs may alert in the field, but subsequent searches may not locate any contraband if the contraband recently was there or residue persists. Such alerts are not actually false positives, and using them to attack a dog's reliability is not as probative of reliability as records of the dog's performance in carefully controlled circumstances in periodic training and certification testing.[9]

### BAILEY V. UNITED STATES, 133 S.CT. 1031 (2013)

In this case the Court clarified its decision in *Michigan v. Summers,* which established the authority of police to detain persons found at the scene during the execution of a search warrant.[10] In *Summers,* police were approaching a house to execute a search warrant for illegal drugs just as the defendant, Summers, was walking down the front steps. Police detained Summers as they executed the warrant, and he was arrested when narcotics were found in the course of the search. The Court found that the limited detention was a seizure, but that it was reasonable. The Court reasoned that the detention furthered legitimate government interests to include facilitating the orderly completion of the search, ensuring officer safety, and preventing escape in the event incriminating evidence is found during the search.[11]

In *Bailey* police were watching a house in anticipation of executing a search warrant for a gun based on informant information indicating that the gun belonged to a drug dealer known as "Polo," who lived at the house.[12] Two men matching the description of Polo left the home and were followed by police as they drove away from the house. Five minutes after they left the residence, the men were stopped, detained, and questioned about a mile away. The Court held this detention was not reasonable, distinguishing it from *Summers.*

The Court stated the important law enforcement interests underlying the *Summers* rule as applied to persons found on the premises where a search warrant is being executed do not apply with the same or similar force to the detention of recent occupants beyond the immediate vicinity of the premises to be searched. Each interest on its own also is insufficient to justify an expansion of the rule in *Summers* to permit the detention of a former occupant, wherever he may be found, away from the scene of the search.[13]    Therefore,    the    authority    outlined in *Summers* to detain persons at the scene where a search warrant is being executed is limited to the immediate vicinity of the search.

### *MISSOURI V. MCNEELY*, 133 S.CT. 1552 (2013)

In *McNeely* the government sought a blanket exception to the warrant requirement for nonconsensual blood testing in DUI cases on the theory that the natural metabolization of alcohol in the human body (and thereby the destruction of evidence) constituted an exigent circumstance. In *Schmerber v. California*[14] the defendant had been in a serious car accident that injured himself and others and was at the hospital about 2 hours later when the arresting officer had a doctor take a nonconsensual blood draw.

While expressly limiting the ruling to the facts of that case, the *Schmerber* Court held that the police officer there    reasonably    might    have    believed    he    was confronted with an emergency in which the delay necessary    to    obtain    a    warrant    under    the circumstances threatened the destruction of evidence because the human body functions to eliminate alcohol from the system.[15]

The *Schmerber* Court noted that the determination an exigency existed was made under the particular facts of that case—notably, that time already had been taken to bring the defendant to a hospital for treatment and to investigate the scene of the accident.[16]

The Supreme Court in *McNeely* declined to apply a finding of exigency based on the human body metabolizing alcohol—thus, destroying evidence—to all cases. In *McNeely* the defendant was pulled over for traffic violations, appeared intoxicated, and did poorly on field sobriety tests. The defendant refused to take a breathalyzer test and was taken to a hospital where a nonconsensual blood draw was taken less than half an hour after he was stopped.[17]

The Supreme Court held the determination of whether an exigency existed excusing the need to obtain a warrant must in each case be based on the totality of the circumstances. The Court reasoned against a categorical finding of exigency by noting there will be circumstances where getting a warrant will not cause a delay in testing the blood alcohol content of the defendant and also that blood alcohol content evidence is lost at a gradual and relatively predictable rate.

The Court also importantly acknowledged technological advances in the 47 years since it decided *Schmerber,* taking notice of the fact officers can use cellular phones and electronic applications to obtain warrants resulting in some instances in the process causing little or no delay to the collection of evidence.[18] This acknowledgement by the Court that technology has made the warrant application process more expedient likely will be applied going forward in other situations where the government contends an exigent circumstance justifies an exception to the rule requiring a warrant for a search.

### *MARYLAND V. KING,* 133 S.CT. 1958 (2013)
The Supreme Court again had to deal with the impact of changing technology under the Fourth Amendment in *Maryland v. King.* This case was a challenge to Maryland's law requiring that buccal swab DNA samples be taken as a routine part of booking for

serious offenses. King was arrested in 2009 and booked on an assault charge. As part of standard booking procedure under Maryland law, a swab of his inner cheek was taken to obtain skin cells for a DNA test. King's DNA was run against a database of unsolved crimes, and he was connected to an unsolved rape in 2003 for which he later was convicted.[19] In a 5 to 4 decision, the Court decided such DNA testing was permissible under the Fourth Amendment.

The Court referenced the safeguards in the statute in support of its ruling. For example, the Maryland statute provides the DNA sample is not to be processed or placed in a database until there is an arraignment and a judicial officer ensures there was probable cause for arrest. If no probable cause exists or the prosecution does not result in a conviction, the sample is to be destroyed.[20] The law also contains protections limiting the uses of the DNA, prescribing it may only be used for identification purposes,[21] and tests for familial matches are not permitted.[22]

The court found that under the statute DNA was obtained in a minimally intrusive manner, and the collection was justified by the government interest in processing and identifying persons law enforcement officers have taken into custody. Fully identifying persons in custody, to include their criminal history—known and unknown—was important in making decisions regarding the safety risk such persons pose while in custody, the level of security to which they should be subject, and whether to grant bail. In other words, if persons arrested for burglary can, in fact, be implicated in a rape by their DNA, they should be handled while in custody with a level of security befitting their more serious crime, and bail decisions regarding the safety of the community and likelihood of flight should consider the more serious crime to which the individuals are linked.[23]

The Court further reasoned that a person's DNA profile was another facet of their identity, like their fingerprints, photographs, or tattoos. The collection of such information incident to arrest to serve the government interest in identifying arrestees long has been held reasonable,[24] and DNA simply is a more effective means of identification. The Maryland statute, with limitations on the collection and use of DNA obtained from arrestees, is reasonable under the Fourth Amendment.[25]

### *SALINAS V. TEXAS,* 133 S.CT. 2174 (2013)

Salinas was a suspect in the shotgun murders of two brothers. Police visited him at his home, and he surrendered a shotgun for ballistics testing. Salinas also agreed to voluntarily accompany police to the station for questioning. All parties agree the interview was noncustodial for *Miranda* purposes. The interview lasted about an hour. For most of the interview, petitioner answered the officers' questions. But, when asked whether ballistics tests would match his shotgun to the shells recovered at the scene of the murder, Salinas did not answer.[26]

Instead of responding, Salinas looked down at the floor, shuffled his feet, bit his bottom lip, clenched his hands in his lap, and began to tighten up.[27] After a few moments of silence, the officer asked additional questions, which Salinas answered.[28]

At trial the police officers testified regarding Salinas not providing a response to their question regarding the ballistics test, and his failure to respond was mentioned in the government's closing argument. Salinas was convicted and appealed, contending the government's use of testimony regarding his remaining silent in response to the question regarding whether ballistic tests would match his guns to the shells from the murder violated his Fifth Amendment rights.

In a 5 to 4 decision, the Court held that Salinas' silence in reaction to the question could be used against him because he did not expressly invoke the privilege against self-incrimination. The Court noted it long has been settled that the privilege is not self-executing, and a witness who seeks the protection of the privilege must claim it.[29]

The Court has acknowledged two exceptions to this rule. A defendant at trial has an absolute right not to testify, and because the defendant's reasons for exercising that right are irrelevant, a requirement for the defendant to expressly invoke the privilege serves no purpose.[30]

The second exception is where governmental coercion makes forfeiture of the privilege involuntary, such as in an un-Mirandized custodial interrogation.[31] Neither of these two recognized exceptions to the requirement a witness expressly invoke the Fifth Amendment applies in this case.

Salinas asked the Court to adopt a third exception to the express invocation requirement where a defendant stands mute and declines to give an answer. The Court noted a defendant could have any number of reasons for remaining silent—for example, to buy time to think up a lie, to protect someone else, or because they are embarrassed. While the Fifth Amendment guarantees that no persons may be compelled to be a witness against themselves, it does not establish an unqualified right to remain silent.[32] The court stated, "A witness' constitutional right to refuse to answer questions depends on his reasons for doing so, and courts need to know those reasons to evaluate the merits of a Fifth Amendment claim."[33]

In response to an invocation of the privilege, the government may either argue the testimony would not incriminate the witness or grant immunity. But, without an express invocation, the government is left to guess at the reason for the witness' silence. Therefore, the Court declined to adopt Salinas' proposed third exception to the rule that an invocation of a witness' right against self-incrimination must be expressly stated. Therefore, the government may comment at trial on a defendant's refusal to answer questions outside of trial where the defendant did not expressly invoke the Fifth Amendment and where there has not been an involuntary forfeiture of the privilege due to government coercion.

### VANCE V. BALL STATE UNIVERSITY, 133 S.CT. 2434 (2013)

In a case of interest from an employment law perspective, the Court defined who is a "supervisor" for purposes of vicarious liability in workplace harassment cases. Vance was employed in a university catering department and alleged racial harassment by a coworker. Under Title VII, if the harasser is merely a coworker, the employer may be liable for a racially hostile work environment if it was negligent in allowing it to persist (i.e., the employer knew or should have known about the hostile environment and failed to take remedial action).[34]

On the other hand, if the harasser is a supervisor, the employer is vicariously liable, but may be able to avail itself of certain defenses.[35] Therefore, the initial step in analyzing the employer's potential liability is determining if the alleged harasser is a supervisor or a mere coworker.

The Court held that someone is considered a supervisor for purposes of determining Title VII liability only when the employer has empowered that employee to take tangible employment actions against the victim (i.e., to effect significant changes in employment status, such as hiring, firing, promoting, reassigning with significantly different responsibilities, or making a decision that causes a significant change in benefits).[36] The coworker who was the alleged harasser was another catering specialist who worked with Vance in the kitchen.

While that coworker was alleged to be one of the leaders in the kitchen and sometimes assigned work or directed other people, she did not have the authority to take any of these more significant tangible actions against Vance, which the Court identified as denoting supervisory status.[37] The court noted this definition of who qualified as a supervisor was simpler than having, in each instance, to consider the whole spectrum of ways in which coworkers interact with each other and that in many instances, the question of supervisor status could be determined before trial as a matter of law.[38]

## CASES OF INTEREST FOR 2013 TO 2014 TERM

*FERNANDEZ V. CALIFORNIA*, CASE BELOW *PEOPLE V. FERNANDEZ*, 208 CAL.APP.4TH 100 (CT. APP. 2012), CERT. GRANTED, 133 S.CT. 2388 (2013)

This case will address the unanswered question left by the Supreme Court's ruling in *Georgia v. Randolph,*547 U.S. 103 (2006). In *Randolph* the court held that where police receive consent to search a residence from one of the co-occupants, but the other co-occupant is present at the time and objects to the police searching the premises, absent exigent circumstances the warrantless search cannot be justified as reasonable as to the objecting co-occupant.[39] In *Fernandez v. California,* Fernandez was present and objected to the police searching his residence, but he then was arrested and taken away. After Fernandez was taken away, a co-occupant gave consent for police to search their common residence, and they found incriminating evidence against Fernandez.[40] The court will decide if

Fernandez' objection to the search had any effect once he no longer was present at the scene of the search.

*KALEY V. UNITED STATES,* CASE BELOW 677 F.3D 1316 (2012), CERT. GRANTED, 133 S.CT. 1580 (2013)

In *Kaley* the defendants were indicted for transportation of stolen property and money laundering. Some of their assets listed in a forfeiture count of the indictment were restrained under a protective order prior to trial. The Kaleys argued that they needed some of those assets to retain counsel of their choice and that freezing their assets violated their Fifth Amendment due process right and their Sixth Amendment right to counsel. The Kaleys sought a hearing prior to trial in which they could challenge the factual basis underlying the grand jury's probable cause determination.[41]

The Eleventh Circuit found they were not entitled to such a hearing because it would amount to giving them two trials on the merits.[42] The Court will determine if defendants are entitled to a hearing when assets are frozen prior to trial to determine not just if the assets frozen are adequately tied to the charges in the indictment but to challenge the indictment on the facts.

*Law enforcement officers of other than federal jurisdiction who are interested in this article should consult their legal advisors. Some police procedures ruled permissible under federal constitutional law are of questionable legality under state law or are not permitted at all.*

ENDNOTES

[1] *United States v. Jones,* 132 S.Ct. 945 (2012).
[2] See *Oliver v. United States,* 466 U.S. 170 (1984).
[3] *Katz v. United States,* 389 U.S. 347 (1967).
[4] *Florida v. Jardines,* 133 S.Ct. at 1415-1416.
[5] *Id.* at 1416.

[6] Three concurring justices also would have found the drug dog's sniff at the door to have been a violation of the defendants' reasonable expectation of privacy under *Katz v. United States,* 389 U.S. 347 (1967) and, therefore, a search on both grounds. *Florida v. Jardines,* 133 S.Ct. 1409, 1418-1420.

[7] *Florida v. Harris,* 133 S.Ct. 1050, 1055 (2013).

[8] *Id.* at 1056.

[9] *Id.* at 1056-1057.

[10] *Michigan v. Summers,* 452 U.S. 692 (1981).

[11] *Id.* at 702-703.

[12] *Bailey v. United States,* 133 S.Ct. 1031, 1036 (2013).

[13] *Id.* at 1041.

[14] *Schmerber v. California,* 384 U.S. 757 (1966).

[15] *Id.* at 770.

[16] *Id.* at 770-771.

[17] *Missouri v. McNeely,* 133 S.Ct. 1552, 1556-1557 (2013).

[18] *Id.* at 1561-1562.

[19] *Maryland v. King,* 133 S.Ct. 1958, 1965 (2013).

[20] *Id.* at 1967.

[21] The Court noted the DNA loci tested under the statute does not contain or reveal genetic traits of the person who supplied the sample, such as genetic disease, predisposition to medical conditions, or heredity. *Id.* at 1979-1980.

[22] *Id.* at 1967.

[23] *Id.* at 1972-1973.

[24] *Id.* at 1970-1971.

[25] The court in its opinion noted that all 50 states and the Federal government collect DNA from felony convicts. *Id.* at 1968. The Maryland statute upheld here allows DNA to be collected from persons arrested for crimes of violence and certain other serious crimes. *Id.* at 1967. The question remains whether a statute allowing DNA collection for arrests or convictions for less serious crimes would be found to be reasonable under the Fourth Amendment in light of the governmental interests being balanced against personal privacy interests.

[26 *Salinas v. Texas,* 133 S.Ct. 2174, 2178 (2013).

[27] *Id.* at 2178.

[28] *Id.* at 2178.

[29] *Id.* at 2178, citing to *Minnesota v. Murphy,* 465 U.S. 420, 425, 427 (1984), quoting from *United States v. Monia,* 317 U.S. 424, 427 (1943).
[30] *Id.* at 2179.
[31] *Id.* at 2180.
[32] *Id.* at 2182-2183.
[33] *Id.* at 2183.
[34] See *Burlington Industries, Inc. v. Ellerth,* 524 U.S. 742, 760 (1998).
[35] *Id.* at 764-765.
[36] *Vance v. Ball State University,* 133 S.Ct. 2434, 2443 (2013).
[37] *Id.* at 2439.
[38] *Id.* at 2450.
[39] *Georgia v. Randolph,* 547 U.S. 103, 120 (2006).
[40] *People v. Fernandez,* 208 Cal.App.4th 100,106 (Ct. App. 2012).
[41] *Kaley v. U.S.,* 677 F.3d 1316, 1317 (2012).
[42] *Id.* at 1327.

## CRITICAL THINKING EXERCISE

Let's take a closer look at the case of *Bailey v. United States,*
133 S.Ct. 1031 (2013). I don't think the Court held that the
stop and detention a mile away was improper altogether (as
stated in the article), but only in its application to *Summers.*
The officers found no weapons or contraband on the
individuals or in their vehicle. I have done this hundreds of
times, and often with as little information as the officers had
in this case. Frequently, I seized weapons, drugs, or evidence
of other crimes. In some instances I found the occupants to
have been wanted for criminal offenses or to have been
fugitives from justice. But what appears to have gone wrong
in this case was the fact that the officers—having found
nothing—transported the men back to the apartment where
a search was underway. It is implied in the case that a
warrant had actually been executed by that time, and the
police had discovered a firearm and illegal drugs in the
apartment. Both men were arrested, and Bailey's keys were
seized incident to the arrest. One of his keys was found to fit
the apartment door; thus, providing more evidence relative
to the actual or constructive possession of the drugs and the
gun. As previously noted, the Supreme Court held that
*Summers* did not apply in this case; the detention on the
scene, after having been brought there from a location one
mile away was not reasonable. Accordingly, the key, which
was the result of Bailey's improper detention and subsequent
arrest, was inadmissible as evidence against him.

Discuss how the police might have handled this situation
differently. Also examine how the prosecutor might have
argued cases such as *United States v. Ross,* 456 U.S. 798
(1982) and *Michigan v. Thomas,* 458 U.S. 259 (1982). But see
also, the articles on pp. 77 and 105.

# THE EXIGENT CIRCUMSTANCES EXCEPTION AFTER KENTUCKY V. KING

By Michael T. Pettry, J.D.

March 2012: *FBI Law Enforcement Bulletin*

ON A DAILY BASIS, LAW ENFORCEMENT OFFICERS FACE situations requiring them to make split-second decisions under tense, uncertain, and often chaotic circumstances. Fortunately, courts, recognizing the realities of modern policing, have provided officers with the legal guidance they need to deal with myriad situations and also have ensured the protection of individual liberties. However, one issue that lacks a clear consensus is when and under what circumstances police are permitted to rely upon the exigent circumstances exception to the Fourth Amendment's warrant requirement when their actions may have caused the exigency.

In its 2010 term, the Supreme Court in *Kentucky v. King* addressed this issue and in doing so provided law enforcement officers with clear guidance as to how they properly can handle some of the most important issues they confront every day.[1] This article will examine the legal issues implicated by the holding in King, lower courts' previous treatment of this issue, and an explanation of the legal standard the Court set forth for officers confronted with situations requiring immediate entry into areas protected by the Fourth Amendment.

## CONSTITUTIONAL PROTECTIONS

The Fourth Amendment provides: "The right of the people to be secure in their persons, houses, papers, and effects, against unreasonable searches and seizures, shall not be violated, and no Warrants shall issue, but upon probable cause, supported by Oath or affirmation, and particularly describing the place to be searched, and the persons or things to be seized."[2]

Thus, the text of the amendment offers two distinct requirements regarding searches: 1) they must be reasonable and 2) a warrant may not be issued unless probable cause is established and the scope of the search is specified with particularity. Although the amendment does not specifically state when and under what circumstances a warrant must be obtained, the Supreme Court has indicated that "searches and seizures inside a home without a warrant are presumptively unreasonable."[3]

## EXIGENT CIRCUMSTANCES EXCEPTION

In spite of the presumption that a police officer's entry into a home without a warrant is unlawful, both state and federal courts have carved out a number of exceptions to this general rule. Included among the judicially recognized exceptions to the Fourth Amendment's warrant requirement is the exigent circumstances exception. The U.S. Court of Appeals for the First Circuit in *United States v. Rengifo* indicated that "[e]xigent circumstances occur when a reasonable officer could believe that to delay acting to obtain a warrant would, in all likelihood, permanently frustrate an important police objective, such as to prevent the destruction of evidence relating to criminal activity or to secure an arrest before a suspect can commit further serious harm."[4]

## POLICE-CREATED EXIGENCY DOCTRINE

Although the Supreme Court recently had provided clear guidance to law enforcement officers regarding the circumstances under which they could make a warrantless entry of a dwelling to render emergency aid, it had yet to address the specific issue of whether the exigent circumstances exception to the Fourth Amendment's warrant requirement applies when police officers' actions cause the exigency.[5] Under this so-called police-created exigency doctrine, a number of lower courts had held that officers could not rely upon this exception if they had created the very exigency which they sought to use to justify acting without a warrant.[6] Other courts did not find a Fourth Amendment violation simply on the grounds that officers created the exigency.[7]

Given the context in which the issue may arise, this left law enforcement in a difficult predicament given the unsettled nature of the law. The Supreme Court's decision in *King* provides welcome clarification of the circumstances under which law enforcement is permitted to rely upon the exigent circumstances exception.

In *King*, officers in Lexington, Kentucky, arranged for the controlled purchase of crack cocaine outside of an apartment complex.[8] After completion of the deal, an undercover officer monitoring the transaction from a nearby location instructed the uniformed officers with whom he was working to apprehend the suspect. The undercover officer informed his fellow officers that the subject was moving quickly toward the breezeway of a nearby apartment building and that they should "hurry up and get there" before the individual entered an apartment.[9]

After receiving the undercover officer's radio transmission, the uniformed officers drove into the nearby parking lot, exited their vehicles, and ran to the breezeway. As they entered the breezeway, the officers heard the sound of a door shutting and detected the strong odor of burnt marijuana. At the end of the breezeway, the officers discovered that there was an apartment on each side of the hallway. Although the undercover officer who had been monitoring the transaction had alerted the uniformed officers that the subject had entered the apartment on the right, the officers could not hear the transmission as they already had exited their vehicles. The officers focused their attention on the door on the left side of the breezeway as it appeared to be the source of the pungent odor.[10]

The officers then banged on the door "as loud as [they] could" and stated words to the effect of "This is the police" or "Police, police, police."[11] One of the officers later testified at a suppression hearing that as soon as they announced their presence, they could hear people inside the apartment moving and sounds that appeared to reflect that items within were being moved.[12] Believing that the sounds indicated that drug-related evidence was about to be destroyed, the officers announced that they "were going to make entry inside the apartment."[13] One of the officers kicked in the door, and they entered.

Once inside, the officers encountered three people in the front room, including the defendant, Hollis King. While performing a protective sweep of the apartment, the officers saw marijuana and powdered cocaine in plain view. A subsequent search yielded additional drugs, cash, and drug paraphernalia.[14]

Following his indictment for drug-related offenses, King filed a motion to suppress the evidence seized by the officers following their warrantless entry into the apartment. Both the trial court and the Kentucky

Court of Appeals overruled his motion.[15] However, the Supreme Court of Kentucky reversed the lower courts, finding that although the officers did not act in bad faith in entering the apartment, the exigent circumstances exception could not justify the search because it was reasonably foreseeable that the occupants would destroy evidence when the police knocked on the door and announced their presence.[16]

In reaching its decision, the Kentucky Supreme Court adopted a two-part test.[17] The first prong required courts to determine "whether the officers deliberately created the exigent circumstances with the bad faith intent to avoid the warrant requirement."[18] If so, they would be prevented from relying on the resulting exigency to justify the warrantless entry.[19] Even if it was shown that the police had not acted in bad faith, the second prong of the test required courts to examine whether "it was reasonably foreseeable that the investigative tactics employed by the police would create the exigent circumstances relied upon to justify a warrantless entry."[20] If the officers' tactics had created the exigency, the warrantless entry would be unjustified.[21]

The Commonwealth of Kentucky appealed the decision to the Supreme Court, which agreed to hear the case. At the outset of its analysis of the case, the Supreme Court noted that the Fourth Amendment's warrant requirement is subject to certain exceptions, such as when "the exigencies of the situation make the needs of law enforcement so compelling that [a] warrantless search is objectively reasonable under the Fourth Amendment."[22] One such exigency would be the need to prevent the "imminent destruction of evidence."[23]

Although this specific type of exigency has long been recognized by the judiciary, many courts have held that it should not apply in situations where the police "created" the exigency to justify acting outside of the judicial process.

As the U.S. Court of Appeals for the Sixth Circuit stated in its decision in *United States v. Chambers*, "for a warrantless search to stand, law enforcement officers must be responding to an unanticipated exigency rather than simply creating the exigency for themselves."[24] Similarly, the U.S. Court of Appeals for the Fifth Circuit noted in *United States v. Gould* that "although exigent circumstances may justify a warrantless probable cause entry into the home, they will not do so if the exigent circumstances were manufactured by the agents."[25]

Although courts had held that officers could not rely upon the exigent circumstances exception to the warrant requirement if they had created the exigency, they recognized that something more than a general fear of detection or discovery by the police must have caused the destruction of evidence.

As the U.S. Court of Appeals for the Eighth Circuit observed in *United States v. Duchi*, "in some sense the police always create the exigent circumstances that justify warrantless entries and arrests. Their discovery of the criminal causes him to flee; their discovery of the contraband causes the criminal's attempt to destroy or divert the evidence."[26] The Supreme Court recognized this common sense principle in its opinion in *King* by noting that individuals engaged in illegal activity often will destroy evidence if they have concerns that it will be recovered by law enforcement.

In *King*, the Supreme Court recognized the danger in adopting a rule that would prevent the police from relying upon the exigent circumstances exception to prevent the destruction of evidence if their actions had played a role in creating the exigency. The Court noted that although a number of federal and state courts had considered this issue, they had employed multiple tests using different legal theories to decide such cases. In rejecting several of these tests due to their adoption of legal requirements that it characterized as "unsound," the Supreme Court reaffirmed the long-established legal principle that "warrantless searches are allowed when the circumstances make it reasonable, within the meaning of the Fourth Amendment, to dispense with the warrant requirement."[27]

In explaining its reasoning in *King*, the Court examined several of the tests used by courts when presented with challenges to searches under the police-created exigency doctrine. As previously noted, some courts, including the Kentucky Supreme Court, had used a so-called bad faith test. The Court expressly rejected this test as it was "fundamentally inconsistent" with its previous Fourth Amendment decisions.[28]

Those decisions stand for the proposition that the appropriate focus in evaluating the actions of a law enforcement officer under the Fourth Amendment is considering whether the actions are objectively reasonable at the time they are taken, not the subjective motivations of the officer.

The Court also examined the use of a reasonable foreseeability test, such as that relied upon by the Supreme Court of Kentucky in its decision finding that the Lexington officers had improperly created an exigency to gain entry into the apartment. In its criticism of the reasonable foreseeability test, the Supreme Court noted it previously had rejected the notion that "police may seize evidence without a warrant only when they come across the evidence by happenstance."[29]

For example, in the oft-cited case of *Horton v. California*, the Supreme Court held that police may seize evidence in plain view even though an officer may be "interested in an item of evidence and fully expects to find it in the course of a search."[30]

The Court also was concerned that the use of a reasonable foreseeability test to evaluate officers' actions under the exigent circumstances exception would lead to an unacceptable degree of unpredictability. Rather than focusing on whether the officers' actions were objectively reasonable at the time they were taken, courts instead would be required on a case-by-case basis to "quantify the degree of predictability that must be reached before the police-created exigency doctrine comes into play."[31]

Such an approach likely would create "unacceptable and unwarranted difficulties for law enforcement officers who must make quick decisions in the field, as well as for judges who would be required to determine after the fact whether the destruction of evidence in response to a knock on the door was reasonably foreseeable based upon what the officers knew at the time."[32]

Another test used by courts applying the police-created exigency doctrine focused on whether the officers acted without a warrant even after they had developed sufficient probable cause to search a specific location. Such situations sometimes arise with a so-called knock-and-talk scenario where the police knock on the door of a particular residence and ask to speak with an occupant or seek consent to search. In rejecting such an approach, the court recognized that "there are many entirely proper reasons why police may not want to seek a search warrant as soon as the bare minimum of evidence needed to establish probable cause is acquired."[33]

The Court further added that "[f]aulting the police for failing to apply for a search warrant at the earliest possible time after obtaining probable cause imposes a duty that is nowhere to be found in the Constitution."[34]

Finally, the Supreme Court rejected a test used by some lower courts that would deprive officers of the ability to rely upon the exigent circumstances exception when it is determined that their investigation departed from "standard or good law enforcement practices."[35] In its criticism of this test, the Court noted that not only would it fail to provide clear guidance to law enforcement officers but it also would require an inappropriate after-the-fact analysis of decisions that should remain within the province of law enforcement personnel.[36]

Also, the Court declined to adopt a rule that "law enforcement officers impermissibly create an exigency when they engage in conduct that would cause a reasonable person to believe that entry is imminent and inevitable."[37] King had argued that courts should consider such factors as the officers' tone of voice in announcing their presence and the forcefulness of their knocks.[38] However, the Court noted that such a test likely would interfere with officers' ability to properly respond to an emergency situation as it would require them to consider subtle and ill-defined standards of conduct.[39]

For example, officers would be required to guess as to whether the tone and volume of their voice or the force of their knocking had caused them to violate the police-created exigency rule. Moreover, courts reviewing the officers' conduct would have great difficulty in determining whether the police had crossed some poorly defined and nebulous threshold.

The Court rejected not only the test proposed by *King* but also those used by lower courts to decide police-created exigency issues. The Court first assumed for purposes of argument that exigent circumstances existed at the time the officers made the decision to enter King's apartment without a warrant.[40]

Once this threshold issue was established, the Court needed only to decide the fairly narrow issue of under what circumstances police impermissibly create an exigency.[41] The focus of the Court's analysis was whether the police violated the Fourth Amendment or threatened to do so prior to forcing entry into the apartment. Although the record indicated that the police had banged loudly on the door to the apartment and announced their presence, those actions are not outside the bounds of accepted law enforcement conduct under the Fourth Amendment. The result would have been different had the police threatened the occupants to "open the door or else" or otherwise demanded entry to the apartment.

In holding that the exigent circumstances exception applies as long as the police do not gain entry to premises by means of an actual or threatened violation of the Fourth Amendment, the Court eliminated the confusion inherent in the tests used by the lower courts. The rule announced by the Court clearly allows officers confronted with circumstances, such as those present in *King*, to take appropriate steps to resolve the emergency situation. However, officers must be mindful of the fact that they cannot demand entry or threaten to break down the door to a home if they do not have independent legal authority for doing so. According to the Court, to do so would constitute an actual or threatened violation of the Fourth Amendment and, thereby, deprive the officers of the ability to rely upon the exigent circumstances exception.

## CONCLUSION

The Court's decision in *King* provides much-needed guidance for officers in dealing with many of the situations they encounter on a regular basis. Provided their actions fall within established legal standards of conduct under the Fourth Amendment, officers no longer will have to guess as to whether they impermissibly caused an exigency, thereby depriving them of the ability to take appropriate action. As with all exceptions to the warrant requirement, officers should recognize that the burden remains on the government to justify fully its actions under the Fourth Amendment. Moreover, officers should be aware that their actions may be constrained by other applicable constitutional protections.[42]

## ENDNOTES

[1] 131 S.Ct. 1849 (2011).

[2] U.S. Constitution, Fourth Amendment.

[3] *Brigham City v. Stuart*, 547 U.S. 398, 403 (2006), quoting *Groh v. Ramirez*, 540 U.S. 551, 559 (2004).

[4] 858 F.2d 800, 805 (1st Cir. 1988).

[5] *See Brigham City, supra*; and *Michigan v. Fisher*, 130 S.Ct. 546 (2009). *See also*, Michael T. Pettry, "The Emergency Aid Exception to the Fourth Amendment's Warrant Requirement," *FBI Law Enforcement Bulletin*, March 2011, p. 26.

[6] *See United States v. Munoz-Guerra*, 788 F.2d 295, 298 (5th Cir.1986); United States v. Richard, 994 F.2d 244, 249-250 (5th Cir. 1993); and Mann v. State, 357 Ark. 159, 161 S.W. 3d 826, 834 (Ark. 2004).

[7] See *United States v. MacDonald*, 916 F.2d 766, 772 (2nd Cir. 1990); *State v. Robinson*, 327 Wis.2d, 302, 326-328; and 786 N.W. 2d 463, 475-476 (Wis. 2010).

[8] 131 S.Ct. 1849, 1854 (2011).

[9] *Id.*

[10] *Id.*

[11] *Id.* (internal quotations omitted).

[12] *Id.*

[13] *Id.*

[14] Officers subsequently determined that the subject involved in the drug buy actually had entered the apartment on the right.

[15] *Id.* at 1855.

[16] *King v. Commonwealth*, 302 S.W.3d 649, 656 (Kentucky, Jan. 21, 2010).

[17] *Id.*

[18] *Id.*

[19] *Id.*

[20] *Id.*

[21] *Id.*

[22] *King,* at 1856 (internal quotations omitted).

[23] *Id.*

[24] 395 F.3d, 563, 566 (6th Cir. 2005).

[25] 364 F.3d 578, 590 (5th Cir. 2004) (internal quotations omitted).

[26] 906 F.2d 1278, 1284 (8th Cir. 1990).

[27] *King* at 1858.

[28] *Id.* at 1859.

[29] *Id.*

[30] 496 U.S. 128, 138 (1990).

[31] *King* at 1859.

[32] *Id.* at 1860.

[33] *Id.*

[34] *Id.* at 1861.

[35] *Id.*

[36] *Id.*

[37] *Id.*(internal quotations omitted).

[38] *Id.*

[39] *Id.*

[40] *Id.* at 1862.

[41] *Id.*

[42] Officers should note that although their actions may be viewed as reasonable under the Fourth Amendment, an individual still may allege violations of other constitutional guarantees, such as the Equal Protection Clause of the Fourteenth Amendment, if it appears that the actions of law enforcement were motivated by such factors as race or ethnicity.

*Law enforcement officers of other than federal jurisdiction who are interested in this article should consult their legal advisors. Some police procedures ruled permissible under federal constitutional law are of questionable legality under state law or are not permitted at all.*

## DISCUSSION QUESTION

Assume that the police have probable cause to believe narcotics are being sold out of a particular motel room. While under surveillance, the police make an anonymous telephone call informing the suspects that the "police are on their way to the motel!" Almost instantly, from benefit of their adjacent motel room, the officers overhear commotion and a toilet flushing. Based upon the excellent analysis in this article, would the officers violate the Fourth Amendment if they entered the suspect's motel room without a search warrant?

## CRITICAL THINKING EXERCISE

Consider the case, as I have in the past while supervising law enforcement operations and teaching at the police academy, of *California v. Hodari D.*, 499 U.S. 621 (1991). The U.S. Supreme Court held that a fleeing suspect is not considered "seized," for purposes of the Fourth Amendment, until the officer catches him. In this hypothetical scenario, officers with neither probable cause to arrest nor reasonable suspicion to stop (seize), drive their vehicles up to a street corner on which two men they *merely* suspect to be drug dealers, are standing. They slam on their brakes, "jump out" of the vehicle, and give foot chase. The officers intentionally do not catch the suspects until they are observed throwing down what the officers then have probable cause to believe are illegal drugs. The Court has held this to be a lawful activity, because the seizure did not take place until after reasonable suspicion or probable cause had been developed. What if this scenario was taken one step further and the officers—with probable cause—chased the suspect into his home? What if the officers deliberately, and with calculation, did not catch the suspect; thus allowing him to enter his home before following him in?

# Avoiding the Entrapment Defense
## in a Post-9/11 World

By David J. Gottfried, J.D.

January 2012: *FBI Law Enforcement Bulletin*

**M**ICHAEL, A 19-YEAR-OLD COLLEGE STUDENT, WAS BORN and raised in middle America. According to his roommate, Michael has developed a peculiar fascination, almost an obsession, with al Qaeda and its cause. The roommate watches over the next several months as Michael makes numerous comments indicating support for violence against the United States and, in particular, its military forces. This concern increases when he sees an order Michael placed on the Internet for a how-to guide to building a homemade explosive device. Unnerved with Michael's recent attraction to al Qaeda and support for the use of violence, the roommate approaches the local police department to share his observations.

The Joint Terrorism Task Force (JTTF) begins looking at open-source information about Michael. A 20-year-old JTTF informant makes contact with Michael at a fraternity party, and the two men engage in a conversation about the need to teach America another lesson. Michael proudly announces that he willingly would become a martyr in the name of jihad, but that he lacks money with which to pull off a "glorious" event.

A few weeks later, the informant tells Michael that, through his father, he could come up with $50,000 and that he has a source willing to provide enough materials to "take out a city block." Michael's face lights up, and they agree to make a plan.

This fictional scenario bears a striking resemblance to an emerging trend in the United States. Young people, some still in their teenage years and often from upper-middle-class families, have developed a fervor for anti-American sentiment. Since 9/11, law enforcement agencies have identified many such cases, causing a chilling revelation: If these cases represent the ones authorities have become aware of, how many remain undetected?

## PROACTIVE APPROACH

Given this trend, law enforcement agencies face a difficult task. In the aftermath of 9/11, it no longer proves sufficient to solve crimes after people have committed them. Rather, a top priority of law enforcement is preventing another terrorist attack against U.S. interests. The American people expect federal, state, and local law enforcement officers to proactively prevent another terrorist attack, and even one failure is unacceptable.

Law enforcement officials cannot afford to wait for a terrorist plot to mature before they break it up. A delay could enable an unidentified plotter to launch an attack. In other words, law enforcement must, in a controlled manner, divert someone determined to harm the United States and its people into a plot bound to fail from the outset, instead of one that might succeed.

This approach of proactively identifying criminal activity in its infancy raises unique concerns. Can law enforcement officials exploit an individual's mere desire to kill tens of thousands of innocent people and even facilitate the commission of the crime right up until the last second, controlling the unfolding events to ensure that the perpetrators remain unaware they are dealing with undercover agents? Where is the line between an individual's thoughts and desires and criminal activity?

The answer to these questions requires an understanding of an important legal principle— entrapment. Prosecutors will attempt to refute claims of entrapment in the courtroom, but, actually, cases are won or lost in the planning stages of the investigation. In other words, law enforcement officers play a critical role in conducting an investigation in a manner that prevents the successful assertion of entrapment. The consequence of a successful entrapment defense—the acquittal of an otherwise guilty defendant—is unacceptable. Understanding the contours of the entrapment defense and factoring this into the planning phases of an investigation can make the difference between a successful attack on the government's case and a guilty plea.

Certain investigative techniques used by law enforcement raise the likelihood of the assertion of an entrapment defense. Perhaps, the highest probability of an entrapment defense arises in undercover operations. Law enforcement agencies need not shy away from using undercover operations, but they must structure them carefully. Terrorist recruits susceptible to undercover agents also will be susceptible to real terrorists. This shows the importance of undercover agents recruiting these individuals first. Executed properly, undercover operations—even those in which law enforcement provides both the means and the opportunity for an individual to succeed in committing a "terrorist act"—are entrapment proof. This article examines the history of the concept of entrapment and demonstrates the importance of structuring an investigation in anticipation of an entrapment defense.

## ENTRAPMENT

In its most basic form, entrapment occurs when government authorities induce persons to commit a crime they were not predisposed to commit. A successful claim of entrapment in the legal system can result in defendants' acquittal regardless of whether they actually committed the alleged crime.

More precisely, to successfully assert an entrapment defense in federal and most state courts, defendants must show by a preponderance of the evidence (hence the characterization of entrapment as an "affirmative" defense) that officers induced them to commit the crime.[1] Assuming defendants make their showing of inducement, the burden of proof moves to the prosecution, which must prove beyond a reasonable doubt that the defendant was predisposed to commit the crime.[2] Thus, the entrapment defense can fail in one of two ways: 1) the defendant cannot show inducement; or 2) despite a showing of inducement, the government can prove predisposition.[3]

While federal and most state courts follow the definition described above (also known as the "subjective" test), a few states still follow the "objective" test, which focuses solely on the government's actions and the degree of inducement—in other words, how coercive and persuasive the authorities were.[4] The key to the objective test is whether the degree of governmental persuasion would have induced an innocent person to engage in the criminal activity.

For example, in the 1973 case of People of the State of Michigan v. Turner, the defendant had a 3-year friendship with an undercover agent who served as a part-time sheriff's deputy and a part-time truck driver.[5] The defendant responded to the undercover officer's concern about falling asleep at the wheel by providing caffeine pills. Believing that Turner's access to caffeine pills meant he also had access to narcotics, the agent concocted a story that his girlfriend, a drug addict, would break off their relationship unless he provided her with some heroin. After repeated refusals, Turner provided $20 worth of heroin and $17 worth of marijuana. Turner refused to provide more, but offered to bring the agent to his source. The Michigan Supreme Court overturned Turner's 24- to 40-year sentence for possession and sale of heroin and marijuana, finding law enforcement's actions so reprehensible that a conviction should not be tolerated.[6]

## ORIGIN

In 1932, the Supreme Court first recognized the defense of entrapment in Sorrells v. United States, a prohibition-era case.[7] A prohibition agent learned from informants that Sorrells, a factory worker, had a reputation as a "rumrunner." The agent and three acquaintances of Sorrells spent 90 minutes reminiscing with them about World War I and then asked him "if he would be so kind as to get a fellow soldier some liquor." Initially, Sorrells refused, but later provided a half-gallon bottle of whiskey in exchange for $5. He then was arrested for violating the National Prohibition Act.

In his defense, Sorrells said he told the agent several times that he "did not fool with whiskey" before finally giving in and producing the bottle of liquor. In the majority opinion, Justice Hughes wrote, "it is clear that the evidence was sufficient to warrant a finding that the act for which defendant was prosecuted was instigated by the prohibition agent, that it was the creature of his purpose, that defendant had no previous predisposition to commit it but was an industrious, law-abiding citizen, and that the agent lured defendant, otherwise innocent, to its commission by repeated and persistent solicitation in which he succeeded by taking advantage of the sentiment aroused by reminiscences of their experiences in arms in the World War."[8] As a result, the entrapment defense was born.

## INDUCEMENT

The first prong of the entrapment defense requires a demonstration of inducement by law enforcement. A successful showing of inducement generally requires more than merely establishing that an officer approached and requested a defendant to engage in criminal conduct. While evidence that the officer engaged in persuasion, threats, coercive tactics, harassment, or pleas based on sympathy or friendship may prove sufficient in showing inducement, most courts also require the defendant to demonstrate that law enforcement's actions led an otherwise innocent person to commit the crime.[9]

Inducement generally can be categorized in one of two ways. The first involves a situation in which a law enforcement officer makes an essential contribution to the commission of the crime. The second type of inducement involves repeated requests, sometimes made in an atmosphere of camaraderie, that even may include coercion to induce criminal behavior.

In 1973, the Supreme Court permitted the government to participate in the illegal actions in *United States v. Russell.*[10] Joe Shapiro, an undercover agent for what later would become the Drug Enforcement Agency, was assigned to locate an illegal methamphetamine production laboratory in Washington state. His investigation led him to Richard Russell and John and

Patrick Connolly, the laboratory's proprietors. Shapiro went to Russell's home where he learned that the men had been making methamphetamines for 6 months and already had produced 3 pounds of it. The laboratory recently had been dormant because, as Russell told the undercover agent, he had difficulty procuring *phenyl-2-propanone (P2P)*, a legal but rare and essential ingredient in methamphetamines. Shapiro said he could procure P2P and would do so in exchange for half of the laboratory's production. Shapiro provided P2P and, later, received his share of the finished product. At trial, defendants asserted the entrapment defense, calling attention to the fact that Shapiro affirmatively had participated in the plot, even going so far as to point out that without Shapiro's inducement and contribution of P2P, no illegal drugs could have been produced.

The Supreme Court ruled that entrapment had not occurred, noting that neither the fact of deceit (through the undercover operation) nor the fact that government officers afforded an opportunity or facilitated the commission of the offense would defeat the prosecution.[11] The Court stated that only when government deception actually implants criminal design in the mind of a defendant does the defense of entrapment come into play.[12] Simply put, the entrapment defense prohibits law enforcement officers from instigating criminal acts by otherwise innocent persons to lure them to commit crimes and then punish them for the acts.[13]

In 1992, the Supreme Court further examined this issue in *Jacobson v. United States*.[14] In this case, a middle-aged Nebraska farmer with no criminal record lawfully ordered from an adult bookstore two magazines containing photographs of naked teenage boys. In 1984, Congress passed the Child Protection Act of 1984 (CPA), which made it illegal to receive such materials through the mail. The U.S. Postal Service obtained Jacobson's name from a mailing list seized at the adult bookstore and, in January 1985, initiated an undercover operation targeting him. Government agents, using fictitious organizations and a contrived pen pal, contacted Jacobson by mail, making available the opportunity to purchase additional child pornography. The communications also contained disparaging remarks about the legitimacy and constitutionality of efforts made by Congress to restrict the availability of sexually explicit material and, ultimately, offered Jacobson the opportunity to order illegal child pornography. More than 2 years after the initial contact, government agents sent Jacobson a brochure advertising photographs of two teenage boys engaged in sexual activity. In response to this solicitation, Jacobson placed an order. After government agents effectuated the delivery of Jacobson's order, law enforcement officers searched his house, revealing only the magazine the government provided and two other magazines lawfully acquired before the CPA was passed.

Jacobson was charged with receiving child pornography through the mail in violation of federal law.[15] He was convicted, but the Supreme Court, ultimately, overturned the conviction based on Jacobson's claim of entrapment. The Supreme Court held that "law enforcement officers may not originate a criminal design, implant in an innocent person's mind the disposition to commit a criminal act, and then induce commission of the crime so that the government may prosecute."[16]

The inducement in Jacobson in and of itself did not perfect the successful entrapment defense. The prosecution still had an opportunity to prove that the defendant was predisposed to commit the crime. However, this example clearly demonstrates that the more forceful the inducement, the more critical the showing of predisposition becomes.

## PREDISPOSITION

While inducement focuses on the conduct of law enforcement, predisposition focuses on the defendant's actions and statements. Predisposition is a willingness to commit a crime prior to the introduction of any law enforcement inducement. It often is demonstrated by showing a reasonable indication that the defendant has engaged or intends to engage in criminal activity.[17] However, predisposition also can be shown through an overall eagerness to participate in general criminal activity, or a quick response to law enforcement's inducement. In other words, while the predisposition must exist *before* law enforcement's inducement, it may be proved by actions or events in response to inducement.

As with evidence in general, the more indicia of predisposition, the more entrapment-proof the case will be. Arguably, the single best indicia of predisposition is when the defendant has suggested the crime (i.e., a complete absence of any inducement). Other common
factors include:

- prior, recent convictions/arrests for similar conduct;
- having (or bragging about) experience or expertise in the suggested illegal activity;
- associating with or expressing sympathies for terrorists/criminals;
- expecting to profit from the crime (either monetarily or through an increase in perceived status); and
- a quick response to the undercover agent's inducement offer and the absence of any reluctance at either the undercover agent's

mere suggestion to commit the crime or the proposal of other nonviolent alternatives.

For example, in the 2011 case of *U.S. v. Lewis*, the defendant was convicted of conspiring to possess cocaine with intent to distribute and carrying and possessing a firearm during and in relation to a drug trafficking offense.[18] In response to Lewis' assertion of the entrapment defense, the court allowed the prosecution to introduce prior convictions for felonies in possession of a firearm and theft, holding that evidence of previous criminal acts is admissible to prove predisposition "because in such a case the defendant's predisposition to commit the charged crime is legitimately at issue.[19] To be admissible, however, this evidence must show an act that is similar enough and close enough in time to be relevant to the matter at issue."[20]

### UNDERCOVER OPERATIONS

Law enforcement officers play a critical role in preventing a successful entrapment defense. Recognizing that this role starts at the inception of the operation, not in the courtroom, is essential. Using the fictitious example at the beginning of this article, in Michael's case, law enforcement officers could initiate an undercover operation. As part of the operation, the officers may develop a plan, perhaps, created in consultation with prosecutors. This plan could identify both the inducements to be used, as well as how to demonstrate predisposition. In addition, law enforcement officers and attorneys working together could identify specific places during the operation where predisposition may be documented and used in court later.

Finally, law enforcement officers should document each instance where a defendant demonstrates indicia of predisposition. In Michael's case, law enforcement officers could document his conversations with the source, specifically the discussions regarding the need to teach America another lesson, indicating that he willingly would become a martyr in the name of jihad and that he lacked money with which to pull off such an event. Also, the undercover agent may strengthen predisposition by suggesting that Michael use alternatives to violence and reminding him that thousands of innocent women and children would be killed. If these suggestions failed to sway Michael from his stated goal, it should be documented and used to further demonstrate predisposition.

Use of video and audio devices to record communications with undercover officers and cooperating witnesses and to capture observations of the defendant also warrant consideration. It is one thing for a law enforcement officer to testify that the subject was eager to engage in the criminal activity; it is another to hear the eagerness in the subject's voice and see it in the individual's expressions.

## CONCLUSION

In the wake of 9/11, it no longer is enough for law enforcement officers to solve crimes after their commission. Investigative activity that preempts crimes, particularly terrorism in a post-9/11 world, has become commonplace. To help ensure a successful prosecution, law enforcement officers need to recognize the risks associated with proactive investigations and anticipate affirmative defenses, such as entrapment, as they initiate undercover operations. With proper planning and execution, law enforcement officers can use all available tools to prevent another terrorist attack and to help effectively overcome an entrapment defense.

## ENDNOTES

1 *U.S. v. Taylor*, 475 F.3d 65 (2nd Cir. 2007).
2 *U.S. v. Jacobson*, 503 U.S. 540 (1992).

3 *Sherman v. U.S.,* 356 U.S. 369 (1958); *U.S. v. Gendron,* 18 F. 3d 955 (1st Cir. 1994); and *U.S. v. Luisi,* 482 F. 3d 43 (1st Cir. 2007).

4 As of 2011, the following 14 states still follow the "objective" standard for the entrapment defense: Alaska, Arkansas, California, Colorado, Hawaii, Iowa, Kansas, Michigan, New York, North Dakota, Pennsylvania, Texas, Utah and Vermont.

5 390 Mich. 7 (1973).

6 390 Mich. 7 (1973).

7 287 U.S. 435 (1932).

8 *Sorrells v. United States,* 287 U.S. at 438.

9 *U.S. v. Mendoza-Salgado,* 964 F. 2d. 993 (10th Cir. 1992).

10 411 U.S. 423 (1973).

11 *United States v. Russell,* 411 U.S. at 435-436.

12 *Russell,* 411 U.S. at 436.

13 In *Russell,* the Supreme Court raised the possibility that even in a case where predisposition exists, a constitutional challenge based on the Due Process Clause of the Constitution (U.S. Const., Amendment V) still may exist based on the outrageous nature of the government's conduct. The Supreme Court stated, "We may someday be presented with a situation in which the conduct of law enforcement agents is so outrageous that due process principles would absolutely bar the government from invoking judicial process to obtain a conviction." *Russell,* 411 U.S. at 431-432. The Due Process outrageous-government-conduct challenge presents a small opportunity to challenge the government's actions based on the egregious nature of the government's investigative efforts. See, for example, *U.S. v. Twigg,* 588 F. 2d 373 (3rd Cir. 1978) where the government initiated the criminal activity, coerced individuals to engage in it, and provided all the means to carry it out.

14 503 U.S. 540 (1992).

15 Specifically, Title 18, U.S. Code § 2252(a)(2)(A).

16 *Jacobson,* 503 U.S. at 542.

17 *U.S. v. Ortiz,* 804 F.2d 1161,1165 (10th Cir. 1986) (predisposition explores whether defendant was "ready and willing to commit the crime" when approached by law enforcement).

18 641 F. 3d 773 (7th Cir. 2011).

[19] *U.S. v. Swiatek,* 819 F. 2d 721, 728 (7th Cir. 1987).
[20] *Swiatek,* 819 F. 2d at 728.

*Law enforcement officers of other than federal jurisdiction who are interested in this article should consult their legal advisors. Some police procedures ruled permissible under federal constitutional law are of questionable legality under state law or are not permitted at all.*

## Discussion Question

The last statement by the author is spot on. Some states, including the Commonwealth of Pennsylvania, have different laws concerning when a suspect can be audio recorded without their knowledge and consent. Do you know the laws of your state? How can the Fourth Amendment allow the nonconsensual audio recordings during an undercover operation, yet the same activity is prohibited under some state laws?

## Critical Thinking Exercise

The author is absolutely correct when he says, "cases are won or lost in the planning stages of the investigation." In outline form, draw up a list of relevant matters to be covered in the investigative plan in order to ensure that a suspect has not been "entrapped," which by now you should know does not mean setting a lawful "trap." In the end, such a plan may not avoid the assertion of an entrapment defense by the defendant's attorney, but is aimed at successfully overcoming such a defense due to the guilt of the accused and the lawful practice of law enforcement agents. Always bear in mind officer safety!

# Searches of Motor Vehicles

# Incident to Arrest in a Post-Gant World

## By Kenneth A. Myers, J.D.

### April 2011: *FBI Law Enforcement Bulletin*

O N APRIL 21, 2009, THE U.S. SUPREME COURT decided *Arizona v. Gant*,[1] in which the Court announced new, narrow rules as to when law enforcement officers properly may search the passenger compartment of a motor vehicle incident to the arrest of one of its occupants. For approximately 28 years prior to *Gant*, police relied upon the apparent holdings of other U.S. Supreme Court decisions,[2] as well as the holdings of other state and federal precedent, to provide broad justification[3] for searches following the lawful arrest of any occupant, or recent occupant, of a motor vehicle.

However, in *Gant*, the Court limited this Fourth Amendment search authority to two circumstances: "police may search a vehicle incident to a recent occupant's arrest only if the arrestee is within reaching distance of the passenger compartment at the time of the search or it is reasonable to believe the vehicle contains evidence of the offense of the arrest."[4] This article examines how lower courts have interpreted the two-part holding of *Gant* and provide law enforcement officers guidance in conducting future searches of motor vehicles incident to arrest in a post-Gant world.

## SUMMARY OF *GANT*

In *Gant*, Tucson police officers arrested Rodney Gant for driving with a suspended license. After he was handcuffed and locked in the back of a patrol car, officers searched his car and found cocaine in a jacket located on the backseat. Gant moved to suppress the cocaine found on the grounds that the warrantless search of his car violated the Fourth Amendment. The Arizona Supreme Court held that the search-incident-to-arrest exception to the Fourth Amendment's warrant requirement did not justify the search in this case.[5]

The U.S. Supreme Court agreed. Under the facts of the case, Gant was not within reaching distance of the vehicle at the time of the search (he was handcuffed and locked inside a police car), and there was no reason to believe the car contained evidence of the crime for which he was arrested (driving with a suspended license). Therefore, the search of his car violated the Fourth Amendment, and the contraband discovered during the search was suppressed.[6]

## SEARCHES INCIDENT TO ARREST

According to the Supreme Court, searches conducted without a warrant are presumed unreasonable.[7] However, the Court has recognized a "few specifically established and well-delineated exceptions"[8] to the search warrant requirement, to include searches incident to lawful arrest.[9] This exception, as defined by the Court in *Chimel v. California*,[10] "derives from interests in officer safety and evidence preservation that are typically implicated in arrest situations"[11] and is limited to areas within the arrestee's "immediate control."[12] In applying this exception to the motor vehicle context, the Court in *New York v. Belton*[13] held that the area of immediate control is limited to the "passenger compartment of a vehicle and any containers therein as a contemporaneous incident of an arrest of the vehicle's recent occupant."[14] In *Gant*, the Supreme Court clarified that *Belton* tells us what area of the motor vehicle may be searched incident to arrest (scope),[15] while the two-part rule announced in *Gant* establishes when such area may be searched (prerequisite).[16] The Gant test is an either/or proposition, meaning that only one prong of the test must be satisfied to be in compliance with the holding of the decision.[17]

### ACCESS TO PASSENGER COMPARTMENT

The first prong of the holding in *Gant* deals with access and states that "police may search a vehicle incident to a recent occupant's arrest only if the arrestee is within reaching distance of the passenger compartment at the time of the search."[18] This part of the Gant holding is tethered to the Court's decision in *Chimel v. California*[19] and is based on the "safety and evidentiary justifications" of *Chimel's* "reaching-distance rule."[20]

To understand when an arrestee is outside of the reaching distance of the passenger compartment of a motor vehicle, it is best to start with the facts of Gant. In Gant, the defendant was arrested, handcuffed, and locked in the back of a police patrol car at the time that his vehicle was searched.[21]Under these circumstances, the Court determined that the defendant had no access to his vehicle and that the search of his vehicle incident to his arrest was unreasonable under the first prong of the *Gant* test.[22]

Clearly, if an individual has been arrested, placed in handcuffs, and secured in a police vehicle, the first prong of *Gant* does not permit law enforcement officers to conduct a search incident to arrest of the passenger compartment of that individual's motor vehicle as the individual no longer has access to the vehicle. Courts interpreting the Supreme Court's ruling agree that searches incident to arrest under these circumstances would be unreasonable under the first prong of *Gant*.[23]

However, if there are multiple occupants in a vehicle and one occupant is arrested, handcuffed, and secured in a police vehicle, the search of the passenger compartment of the vehicle nevertheless may be permissible incident to arrest if the other occupants still have access to the vehicle. For example, in *United States v. Davis*,[24] the Eighth Circuit Court of Appeals upheld the search of the passenger compartment of a vehicle incident to arrest of the driver when the three remaining, unsecured, and intoxicated occupants "were standing around a vehicle redolent of recently smoked marijuana." According to the court, the facts presented in this case are "textbook examples of '[t]he safety and evidentiary justifications underlying *Chimel's* reaching distance rule....'").[25]

Outside of a *Gant*-like fact pattern, where the arrestee is handcuffed and placed in the back of a patrol car, the analysis under this first prong of *Gant* becomes more challenging. Some of the difficulty derives from the language used in the majority's decision in *Gant*.

In several parts of the decision, the Court refers to whether the arrestee is "secured"[26] or "unsecured"[27] and within access of the vehicle at the time of the search when analyzing the first part of the test. Moreover, in a footnote, the Court explains that "[b]ecause officers have many means of ensuring the safe arrest of vehicle occupants, it will be the rare case in which an officer is unable to fully effectuate an arrest so that a real possibility of access to the arrestee's vehicle remains."[28]

However, when announcing the holding of the decision (and articulating the new two-part rule), the Court dropped any reference to the arrestee being secured or unsecured and simply stated (under the first prong of the test) that police "may search a vehicle incident to a recent occupant's arrest only if the arrestee is within reaching distance of the passenger compartment at the time of the search."[29]

In *Boykins v. State,*[30] the Court of Appeals of Georgia interpreted this first prong of the *Gant* rule "to mean that the police may conduct a search of the passenger compartment of the arrestee's vehicle incident to his lawful arrest in the 'rare case' in which the arrestee has a 'real possibility of access' to his vehicle."[31] In analyzing *Gant,* the court emphasized that the requirement that the arrestee be "unsecured" was "noticeably absent" from the Supreme Court's first prong of the rule.[32]

In *Boykins,* the defendant had been arrested on an outstanding probation warrant, handcuffed, and stood outside of his vehicle under the control of a policeman when his vehicle was searched by another officer. The Court noted that "the trial court apparently inferred from the officer's testimony that *Boykins* was within arm's reach of the passenger compartment"[33] at the time of the search. The Court then distinguished *Gant,* reasoning that "unlike the defendant in *Gant, Boykins* had not been placed in the back of the patrol car at the time of the search; he was standing outside of his vehicle."[34]

Accordingly, in affirming Boykin's conviction for possession of cocaine (which was found in the passenger compartment of his vehicle during the search incident to arrest), the Court held that "whether he [*Boykins*] had any 'real possibility of access' to the passenger compartment of his vehicle was a mixed question of fact and law for the trial court to determine. We will not second-guess the trial court's finding that the search was justified under *Gant* and *Chimel* on the basis of officer safety."[35] Similarly, in applying the two-part *Gant* rule to a nonvehicle situation, the Third Circuit Court of Appeals in *United States v. Shakir*[36] held that "a search is permissible incident to a suspect's arrest when, under all the circumstances, there remains a reasonable possibility that the arrestee could access a weapon or destructible evidence in the container or area to be searched.

Although this standard requires something more than a theoretical possibility that a suspect might access a weapon or evidence, it remains a lenient standard."[37] In *Shakir*, the court affirmed the conviction of an individual for armed bank robbery and refused to suppress evidence found in a bag near his feet during a search incident to his arrest.

The court reasoned that "[a]lthough he was handcuffed and guarded by two policemen, Shakir's bag was literally at his feet, so it was accessible if he dropped to the floor. Although it would have been more difficult for Shakir to open the bag and retrieve the weapon while handcuffed, we do not regard this possibility as remote enough to render unconstitutional the search incident to arrest."[38] The court, citing the Fifth Circuit Court of Appeals, explained that handcuffs are not "fail-safe"[39] and "are a temporary restraining device; they limit but do not eliminate a person's ability to perform various acts."[40]

On the other hand, in *State v. Carter*[41] the Court of Appeals of North Carolina ruled that when the defendant had been "removed from the vehicle, handcuffed, and directed to sit on a curb" when the search of the vehicle was conducted, there was "no reason to believe defendant was within reaching distance or otherwise able to access the passenger compartment of the vehicle."[42] Accordingly, the court could not justify the search incident to arrest under the first prong of *Gant*.[43]

Additionally, in *United States v. Chavez*,[44] the U.S. District Court for the Eastern District of California held that when a defendant fled from the site of an attempted arrest, police were not justified to search his vehicle incident to arrest. The subject had eluded the officers, jumped a fence, and was nowhere near the scene when the search of his vehicle was conducted. Moreover, the police were standing by the car to ensure that if the defendant did return, he would not have access to the vehicle.[45]

From these decisions, it is clear that the first prong of the *Gant* test involves "case-by-case, fact specific decision making"[46] by law enforcement as there no longer is any bright-line rule. The first prong of the test hinges on access and requires officers to articulate facts demonstrating that there is a real or reasonable possibility that the defendant can access the passenger compartment to obtain a weapon or destroy evidence at the time of the search.

When an arrestee has been handcuffed and secured in a police vehicle, the justification for a subsequent search incident to arrest of the passenger compartment of the arrestee's vehicle no longer is present under the first prong of the test. However, when the arrestee has been handcuffed but not yet secured in a police vehicle, there is case law in support of permitting the search of the passenger compartment of the arrestee's vehicle incident to arrest for weapons and evidence as long as the arrestee still is within reaching distance of the vehicle. This is not to recommend that officers keep recently arrested subjects near their vehicles so that such searches may be justified as officer safety remains of paramount importance.

## "REASONABLE TO BELIEVE" STANDARD

The second prong of the *Gant* test permits the search of the passenger compartment of a motor vehicle following the arrest of a recent occupant of that vehicle when "it is reasonable to believe the vehicle contains evidence of the arrest."[47] This prong does not deal with access[48] and is not tethered to the holding of *Chimel*.[49] Instead, this prong is "consistent with the holding in *Thornton*"[50] and is based on Justice Scalia's concurring opinion in that case.[51] Additionally, this second prong is "unique to the automobile context."[52]

The key to understanding the second prong of the *Gant* test is to define "reasonable to believe." In *Gant*, the police arrested the defendant for driving with a suspended license.[53] The Court found the subsequent search incident to arrest of the defendant's vehicle to be unreasonable as it was not likely that the police would discover offense-related evidence during the search.[54]

The Court explained that "[i]n many cases, as when a recent occupant is arrested for a traffic violation, there will be no reasonable basis to believe the vehicle contains relevant evidence...[b]ut in others, including *Belton* and *Thornton*, the offense of the arrest will supply a basis for searching the passenger compartment of an arrestee's vehicle and any containers therein."[55] Of note, both *Belton*[56] and Thorton[57] involved arrests for drug offenses.

The majority in *Gant* did not provide further explanation or guidance as to the second prong of the test. As stated by Justice Alito in his dissenting opinion, this "creates a host of uncertainties."[58] Not surprisingly, lower courts have struggled with the language of this part of the test and have come up with myriad interpretations.

An analysis of these lower court opinions reveals some commonalities. First, the courts generally have not interpreted the "reasonable to believe" standard as being synonymous with probable cause. The vast majority of courts interpreting *Gant* have concluded that the standard is less than probable cause, reasoning that a probable cause standard merely would duplicate the level of proof required under the motor vehicle exception.[59]

However, if the standard is not probable cause, what is it? Courts interpreting this part of the test are not in agreement.[60] There has been a wide range of explanations of the test,[61] but most courts conclude that "reasonable to believe" is determined in one of two ways: 1) by a reasonable suspicion standard or 2) by the nature of the offense. It should be noted that Justice Alito, who dissented in *Gant*, has described this test as a "reasonable suspicion requirement."[62]

In *United States v. Vinton*,[63] the D.C. Court of Appeals presumed that "'the reasonable to believe' standard probably is akin to the 'reasonable suspicion' standard required to justify a Terry[64] search."[65] In applying the standard to the facts of the case, the court justified the search of a locked briefcase found in the passenger compartment of a defendant's vehicle after he was arrested for the unlawful possession of a weapon and the officer had discovered other weapons in the vehicle during a protective search of the passenger compartment.

In *People v. Chamberlain*,[66] the Supreme Court of Colorado, en banc, concluded that the "reasonable to believe" standard of *Gant* requires "some degree of articulable suspicion," similar to the "lesser degree of suspicion commensurate with that sufficient for limited intrusions, like investigatory stops."[67] The court reasoned that the "'nature-of-the-offense' exception, in which a reasonable belief is held to exist whenever the crime of arrest is one for which evidence is possible and might conceivably be found in the arrestee's vehicle...would suffer from objections similar to those that *Gant* condemned in the broad reading of *Belton*."[68]

In *Chamberlain*, the court upheld the suppression of evidence found in the defendant's vehicle after she had been arrested for false reporting; when the officer already possessed her driver's license, registration, and proof of insurance; and it was not reasonable that her vehicle would contain any additional evidence of the offense of the arrest.[69]

A second line of cases interprets "reasonable to believe" as a "nature-of-the-offense" test. This test originates from the Court's language in *Gant*, where the Court explained that there are some offenses, like traffic violations, where "there will be no reasonable basis to believe the vehicle contains relevant evidence."[70]

The Court then cited as examples *Atwater v. Lago Visa*[71] (involving an arrest for "driving without [a] seatbelt fastened, failing to secure [passenger] children in seatbelts, driving without a license, and failing to provide proof of insurance")[72] and *Knowles v. Iowa*[73] (involving an arrest for speeding). The Court stated that in other cases, like *Belton*[74] and *Thornton*[75] (both involving drug arrests), the "offense of arrest will supply a basis for searching the passenger compartment of an arrestee's vehicle and any containers therein."[76]

The Court then concluded that since *Gant* was arrested for driving with a suspended license, the police could not expect to find evidence of this crime in the passenger compartment of his vehicle.[77]

A significant number of lower courts have used the above language to conclude that the second prong of *Gant* hinges on the "nature of the offense" involved in the arrest and "not some independent evidence that gives rise to a belief that the particular vehicle contains evidence."[78] With this test in mind, it is important to examine what types of offenses courts have determined would fall within the parameters of the test. Clearly, most routine traffic offenses fall outside this second prong of *Gant*.[79]

However, courts have justified searches incident to arrest under the "nature of the offense" test for the following offenses: theft,[80] drug offenses,[81] illegal firearms,[82] driving under the influence,[83] and fraud and abuse.[84] It must be remembered that this search authority is limited to evidence of the crime for which the arrest was made "or of another crime that the officer has probable cause to believe occurred."[85]

CONCLUSION
While the U.S. Supreme Court has limited the ability of law enforcement to search the passenger compartment of a motor vehicle incident to the arrest of a recent occupant of that vehicle, it certainly has not eliminated this viable search warrant exception. However, officers applying this exception must be familiar with the wording and meaning of the Court's two-part test articulated in *Gant*. It also must be remembered that facts satisfying either prong of the test will result in a reasonable search incident to arrest.

Under the first prong, the defendant still must have a real possibility of access to the vehicle at the time of the search for this part of the test to be satisfied. This has become a fact-specific, case-by-case determination for the officer to make at the scene of the arrest. Factors in this analysis include whether or not the subject is handcuffed, or secured in a police vehicle, the proximity of the subject to the vehicle to be searched, and subject-to-officer ratio.

If the arrestee no longer has access to the passenger compartment of the vehicle, the officer must determine if it is reasonable to believe that evidence of the offense of the arrest is located in the passenger compartment of the vehicle to be searched. Courts have differed in their interpretation of this second prong of the test, and, until the Supreme Court specifically addresses this issue, it is incumbent on law enforcement officers to learn and follow the precedent of their respective jurisdictions. The two most common interpretations of the second prong of the test are the reasonable suspicion standard and the nature-of-the-offense test.

Even if both prongs of the *Gant* test are inapplicable, a search of a passenger compartment of a motor vehicle still would be considered reasonable if the officer obtains a warrant or follows the prerequisite and scope of another recognized search warrant exception.[86] While the holding of *Gant* restricted searches incident to arrest, it had no impact on the other exceptions, such as consent,[87] the emergency exception,[88] the motor vehicle exception,[89] and the inventory exception.[90]

## ENDNOTES

[1] 556 U.S. ——, 129 S. Ct. 1710 (2009).

[2] In *New York v. Belton*, 453 U.S. 454, 460, 101 S. Ct. 2860, 2864 (1981), the U.S. Supreme Court held that "when a policeman has made a lawful custodial arrest of the occupant of an automobile, he may, as a contemporaneous

incident of that arrest, search the passenger compartment of that automobile." In *Thornton v. United States*, 541 U.S. 615, 124 S. Ct. 2127 (2004), the Court extended the holding of *Belton* to allow for the lawful search of the passenger compartment of a motor vehicle following the arrest of a recent occupant of that vehicle.

[3] *Gant* at 1718-1719.

[4] *Id.* at 1723.

[5] *Id.* at 1714-1716.

[6] *Id.* at 1719. A detailed account of the facts of *Gant* and an in-depth review of the legal precedent leading up to the decision have been the subject of a previous Law Enforcement Bulletin article and will not be repeated herein. See Richard G. Schott, "The Supreme Court Reexamines Search Incident to Lawful Arrest," *FBI Law Enforcement Bulletin*, July 2009. Additionally, the retroactive application of *Gant*, whether police may rely on a "good faith" exception to the exclusionary rule for pre-*Gant* searches, and the extension of *Gant* beyond the motor vehicle context all are beyond the scope of this article.

[7] *Gant* at 1716 (citing *Katz v. United States*, 389 U.S. 347, 357 (1967)).

[8] *Id.*

[9] *Id.*; *Weeks v. United States*, 232 U.S. 383, 392, 34 S. Ct. 341 (1914).

[10] 395 U.S. 752, 763, 89 S. Ct. 2034, 23 L.Ed.2d 685 (1969).

[11] *Gant* at 1716; *United States v. Robinson*, 414 U.S. 218, 230-234, 94 S. Ct. 467 (1973); and *Chimel v. California*, 395 U.S. 752, 763, 89 S. Ct. 2034 (1969).

[12] *Gant* at 1714 (citing *Chimel v. California*, 395 U.S. 752, 763, 89 S. Ct. 2034 (1969)).

[13] 453 U.S. 454, 101 S. Ct. 2860 (1981).

[14] *Gant* at 1715; and *New York v. Belton*, 453 U.S. 454, 460, 101 S. Ct. 2860, 2864 (1981).

[15] *Gant* at 1717-1718, 1724.

[16] Id. at 1724.

[17] Id. ("police may search a vehicle incident to a recent occupant's arrest only if the arrestee is within reaching distance of the passenger compartment at the time of the search or it is reasonable to believe the vehicle contains evidence of the offense of the arrest [emphasis added]). See also United States v. Davis, 569 F.3d 813, 816-

817 (C.A. 8 2009); Commonwealth v. Elliott, 322 S.W.3d
106, 110 (Ky. App. 2010); and Brown v. State, 24 So.3d
671, 678, 34 Fla. L. Weekly D2593 (DC App. Fla. 2009).

18 Id. at 1723.

19 395 U.S. 752, 89 S. Ct. 2034, 23 L.Ed.2d 685 (1969).

20 Gant at 1714.

21 Id. at 1714-1715.

22 Id. at 1719, 1723.

23 See, for example, United States v. Lopez, 567 F. 3d 755,
757-758 (C.A. 6 2009); United States v. Ruckes, 586 F.3d
713 (C.A. 9 2009) (no authority for search incident to arrest
but justified under inventory exception);People v.
Chamberlain, 229 P.3d 1054, 1055 (Colo. 2010); United
States v. Megginson, 340 Fed. Appx. 856, 857 (C.A. 4
2009); State v. Johnson, —-N.C.App.—-, 693 S.E. 2d
711,717 (2010); United States v. Majette, 326 Fed.Appx.
211, 213 (C.A. 4 2009) (unpublished); United States v.
Kelley, 2011 WL 201477 (S.D. Texas 2011); and United
States v. Reagan, 713 F.Supp2d 724, 727 (E.D. Tenn.
2010).

24 569 F. 3d 813 (C.A. 8 2009).

25 Id. at 817. See also United States v. Goodwin-Bey, 584
F.3d 1117, (C.A. 8 2009), cert. denied ___U.S.___, 130 S. Ct.
1563, 176 L.Ed 2d 148 (2010) (permitting search of
passenger compartment of motor vehicle incident to the
arrest of one of the passengers due to safety concern based
on earlier report of a weapon in the vehicle and presence of
three remaining passengers outside of the vehicle. The
three passengers had been patted down, but were not
restrained or otherwise secured); and United States v.
Salamasina, 615 F.3d 925 (C.A. 8 2010) (search of
passenger compartment of vehicle permitted incident to the
arrest of driver on drug charges, even though at time of
search he was handcuffed and moved to a
location next to the patrol car and away from the vehicle.
Defendant's fiancee and two minor children still had access
to the vehicle, and the fiancee repeatedly entered and exited
the vehicle to tend to her children and spoke in a foreign
language to the arrestee despite the officer's instructions
not to do so).

26 Gant at 1714 ("we hold that Belton does not authorize a
vehicle search incident to a recent occupant's arrest after
the arrestee has been secured and cannot access the

interior of the vehicle").

27 Id. at 1719 ("the *Chimel* rationale authorizes police to search a vehicle incident to a recent occupant's arrest only when the arrestee is unsecured and within reaching distance of the passenger compartment at the time of the search").

28 *Supra* note 4.

29 *Id.* at 1724.

30 —-S.E.2d—-, 2010 WL 4243134 (Ga. App. 2010).

31 *Id.* at p. 6.

32 *Id.*

33 *Id.*

34 *Id.*

35 *Id.*

36 616 F.3d 315 (C.A. 3 2010), cert. denied 131 S. Ct. 841 (2010).

37 *Id.* at 321.

38 *Id.*

39 *Id.* at 320.

40 *Id.* (citing *United States v. Sanders*, 994 F.2d 200, 209 (C.A. 5 1993)). See also *United States v. Perdoma*, 621 F.3d 745, 753 (C.A. 8 2010) (without expressly holding that *Gant* applied to nonmotor vehicle situations, the Court reasoned that the fact that the defendant had been handcuffed and restrained by police in a bus terminal at the time of his arrest did not mean that he clearly was outside of reaching distance of his nearby bag at the time of the search).

41 682 S.E.2d 416 (N.C. App. 2009).

42 *Id.* at 421.

43 *Id.*

44 2009 WL 4282111 (E.D. Cal. 2009).

45 *Id.* at p. 5.

46 *Gant* at 1729 (2009) (Alito, J., dissenting).

47 *Id.* at 1724.

48 *United States v. Davis*, 569 F.3d 813, 816-817 (C.A. 8 2009); and *Commonwealth v. Elliott*, 322 S.W.3d 106, 110 (Ky. App. 2010).

49 556 U.S. ——, 129 S. Ct. 1710, 1719 (2009).

50 *Thornton v. United States*, 541 U.S. 615, 124 S. Ct. 2127 (2004) (the U.S. Supreme Court extended the holding of *Belton* to allow for the lawful search of the passenger compartment of a motor vehicle following the arrest of a

recent occupant of that vehicle).

51 *Gant* at 1714, 1719.

52 *Id.*

53 *Id.*

54 *Id.* at 1719.

55 *Id.*

56 453 U.S. 454, 456, 101 S. Ct. 2860, 2864 (1981).

57 541 U.S. 615, 618, 124 S. Ct. 2127 (2004).

58 See *Megginson v. United States*, 129 S. Ct. 1982 (2009) and *Grooms v. United States*, 129 S. Ct. 1981 (2009) (dissenting opinions of Justice Alito in two matters before the Court that were remanded for further consideration in light of *Arizona v. Gant*).

59 See, for example, *United States v. Vinton*, 594 F.3d 14, 25 (DC Cir. 2010), cert. denied 131 S. Ct. 93 (2010);*United States v. Polanco*, —-F.3d.—-, 2011 WL 420747 at * 4 (C.A. 1 2011); *People v. Chamberlain*, 229 P.3d 1054, 1057 (Colo. 2010); *United States v. Leak*, 2010 WL 1418227 (W.D.N.C. 2010); *Powell v. Commonwealth*, 57 Va. App. 329, 339, 701 S.E. 2d 831 (Va. App. 2010); *Idaho v. Cantrell* 233 P.3d 178, 183 (Idaho App. 2010); but, see *United States v. Grote*, 629 F.Supp 2d 1201, 1203 (E.D. Wash.2009) (reasonable to believe equates to probable cause).

60 *State v. Gamboa*, 2010 WL 2773359 (Ariz. App. Div. 1 2010) (unreported).

61 *Id.*

62 *Megginson v. United States*, 129 S. Ct. 1982 (2009).

63 594 F.3d 14 (D.C. Cir. 2010), cert. denied 131 S. Ct. 93 (2010).

64 *Terry v. Ohio*, 392 U.S. 1, 88 S. Ct. 1868, 20 L.Ed.2d 889 (1968).

65 594 F.3d 14, 25 (D.C. Cir. 2010), cert. denied 131 S. Ct. 93 (2010).

66 229 P.3d 1054 (Colo. 2010).

67 Id. at 1057. See also People v. Perez, 231 P.3d 957 (Colo. 2010); *United States v. Reagan*, 713 F.Supp.2d 724, 733 (E.D. Tenn. 2010) (reasonable-to-believe standard is based on common sense factors and the totality of the circumstances that evidence of the offense of the arrest is in the passenger compartment of the vehicle, in other words "particularized and articulable reasons"); *State v. Mbacke*, —-S.E.2d—-, 2011 WL 13814 (N.C. App. 2011) ("we interpret the Supreme Court's holding in *Gant* to require an

officer to suspect the presence of more direct evidence of the crime of arrest than...highly indirect circumstantial evidence...).

68 229 P.3d 1054, 1056-1057 (Colo. 2010).

69 *Id.*

70 *Gant* at 1714, 1719.

71 532 U.S. 318, 324, 121 S. Ct. 1536, 149 L.Ed.2d 549 (2001).

72 *Id.* at 321.

73 525 U.S. 113, 118, 119 S. Ct. 484, 142 L.Ed.2d 492 (1998).

74 *New York v. Belton*, 453 U.S. 454, 460, 101 S. Ct. 2860, 2864 (1981).

75 *Thornton v. United States*, 541 U.S. 615, 124 S. Ct. 2127 (2004).

76 *Gant* at 1714, 1719.

77 *Id.*

78 *Brown v. State,* 24 So.3d 671, 678, 34 Fla. L. Weekly D2593 (D.C. App. Fla. 2009), review denied 39 So.3d 1264 (2010); endnote 79.

79 *United States v. Lopez*, 567 F. 3d 755, 758 (C.A. 6 2009) (reckless driving); *United States v. Brunick*, 374 FedAppx. 714, 716, 2010 WL 1041369 (C.A. 9 2010) (driving under suspended license); *United States v. Ruckes*, 586 F.3d 713,718 (C.A. 9 2009) (driving under suspended license); United States v. Bronner, 2009 WL 1748533 (D. Minn.2009) (driving under revoked license); and *United States v. Holmes*, 2009 WL 1748533 (D. Minn.2009) (unreported) (driving under revoked license).

80 Id. at 677.

81 *United States v. Wright*, 374 Fed.Appx. 386, 391, 210 WL 1500520 (C.A.4 2010); *United States v. Brown*, 2009 WL 2346668 (S.D. Ind. 2009); *United States v. Page*, 679 F.Supp.2d 648 (E.D. Va. 2009); and *United States v. Conerly*, 2010 WL 4723434 (E.D. Mi.2010).

82 *People v. Osborne*, 175 Cal.App.4th 1052, 1065, 96 Ca.Rptr.3d 696 (Cal.App.Dist.1 Div.4 2009).

83 *Commonwealth v. Elliott*, 322 S.W.3d 106, 110 (Ky. App. 2010); *Idaho v. Cantrell*, 233 P.3d 178, 183 (Idaho App. 2010); but see *United States v. Reagan*, 713 F.Supp.2d 724, 733 (E.D. Tenn. 2010) (DUI arrest alone, without particularized and articulable reason to believe evidence of DUI is contained in vehicle at time of search does not

satisfy reasonable-to-believe standard).
84 *United States v. Owen*, 2009 WL 2857959 (S.D. Miss., South. Div. 2009).
85 *Gant* at 1714, 1725 (Scalia, J., concurring); and *Deemer v. State*, —-P.3d.—-, 2010 WL 5187698 (Alaska App. 2010).
86 *Gant* at 1724.
87 *Schneckloth v. Bustamonte*, 412 U.S. 218 (1973).
88 *Schmerber v. California*, 384 U.S. 757 (1966); *Michigan v. Long*, 463 U.S. 1032, 103 S. Ct. 3469, 77 L.Ed.2d 1201 (1983); and *Maryland v. Buie*, 494 U.S. 325, 110 S. Ct. 1093, 108 L.Ed.2d 276 (1990).
89 *United States v. Ross*, 456 U.S. 798, 820-821, 102 S. Ct. 2157, 72 L.Ed.2d 572 (1982); *United States v. Polanco*, —-F.3d.—-, 2011 WL 420747 at * 3 (Co. 1 2011).
90 *South Dakota v. Opperman*, 428 U.S. 364 (1976).

## Discussion Questions

The author states that the *Gant* decision has no effect on other search warrant exceptions relating to motor vehicles, such as the automobile exception and the inventory exception. But do you really think the *Gant* decision had much to do about automobiles in the first instance? What other exception(s) to the search warrant requirement—beyond those connected to automobiles and other motor vehicles—might be affected by *Gant*, if it hasn't already?

## Critical Thinking Exercise

As a team, discuss what police officers should do to comply with *Gant* and at the same time maintain strict officer safety?

# THE SUPREME COURT ANALYZES MAJOR FOURTH AMENDMENT ISSUES IN DOG-SNIFF CASES

By Richard G. Schott, J.D.

June 2013: *FBI Law Enforcement Bulletin*

ON OCTOBER 31, 2012, THE U.S. SUPREME COURT heard oral arguments in two separate cases from Florida, each presenting a different constitutional issue involved in law enforcement agencies' use of drug-sniffing canines. The fact that the Court granted *certiorari* for both cases in the same term and entertained oral arguments for them on the same day caused some pundits to comment that the Court had "gone to the dogs" or had experienced a "dog-day afternoon."[1] These cases, however, because of the underlying issues involved, were no laughing matter to the law enforcement community.

One of the two cases involved whether probable cause—bedrock Fourth Amendment concern—existed at the time law enforcement action (the dog sniff) was taken. The second examined whether a search under the Fourth Amendment even had occurred when a drug-sniffing dog alerted to the presence of contraband outside a homeowner's front door. Clearly, these two cases have the potential to greatly impact how departments employ drug-sniffing canines.

## FLORIDA V. HARRIS

On February 19, 2013, the U.S. Supreme Court decided the first of the two dog-sniffing cases. In *Florida v. Harris* a Liberty County, Florida, Sheriff's Department K-9 officer on patrol with his German shepherd trained to detect certain narcotics pulled over Clayton Harris because the license plate on his truck had expired.[2] When the deputy noticed that Harris was "visibly nervous" (could not sit still and was shaking and breathing rapidly) and had an open can of beer in his truck, he asked for consent to search the vehicle.

When Harris refused, the deputy had the German shepherd, Aldo, perform a "free-air sniff" outside the truck. When Aldo gave a positive alert to the presence of drugs, the deputy concluded that he now had probable cause to search the vehicle, even without Harris' consent.[3] Although the search did not reveal any of the drugs Aldo was trained to detect, it produced 200 loose pseudoephedrine pills; 8,000 matches; hydrochloric acid; antifreeze; and a coffee filter full of iodine crystals, all necessary for making methamphetamine. Subsequently, Harris was charged with possessing pseudoephedrine for use in manufacturing methamphetamine.[4]

Ironically, while Harris was free on bail, the same deputy (again accompanied by his canine partner) pulled Harris over for a traffic violation. Again, Aldo performed a sniff and alerted to the presence of contraband. The deputy again searched Harris' vehicle based on the alert, but located nothing of evidentiary value.[5]

Harris moved to suppress the evidence recovered in the first search on the grounds that the dog alert indicating the presence of narcotics did not provide the deputy with probable cause, which, in turn, had allowed the search. His argument was based not on the quality of training received by Aldo and his handler but on Aldo's certification and performance in the field—particularly, the two stops of Harris' "seemingly narcotics-free" truck.[6] At the hearing to settle the issue, testimony revealed that Aldo's certification (which Florida law did not require) had expired the year before the relevant stop involving Harris and that Aldo's handler did not keep complete records of Aldo's performance in the field. Rather, only records of alerts resulting in arrests were maintained.

After the Florida trial and appellate courts concluded that the dog alert provided probable cause to believe there was evidence in Harris' truck (which, in turn, allowed the search), the Florida Supreme Court reversed the decision, troubled both by what was and was not presented during the suppression hearing. First, according to Florida's highest court, "...the fact that a dog has been trained and certified is simply not enough to establish probable cause."[7]

Rather, that court mandated a rigid checklist approach to satisfying probable cause in such cases, stating: "[T]he state must present...the dog's training and certification records, an explanation of the meaning of the particular training and certification, field performance records (including any unverified alerts), and evidence concerning the experience and training of the officer handling the dog, as well as any other objective evidence known to the officer about the dog's reliability."[8]

The Florida high court was especially concerned with the need for "evidence of the dog's performance history" and "how often the dog has alerted in the field without illegal contraband having been found" because that data could help reveal such problems as a handler's conscious or unconscious tendency to "cue [a] dog to alert" and a "dog's inability to distinguish between residual odors and actual drugs."[9] Because of the rigidity of its test, the Florida Supreme Court mandate would dictate that "an officer...who did not keep full records of his dog's field performance could never have the requisite cause to think 'that the dog is a reliable indicator of drugs.'"[10]

A unanimous U.S. Supreme Court reversed the decision of the Florida Supreme Court. In doing so, the Court relied on its earlier evaluations of the probable cause standard. Justice Elena Kagan, writing for the entire Court, pointed out that "[a] police officer has probable cause to conduct a search when the facts available to him would warrant a person of reasonable caution in the belief that contraband or evidence of a crime is present."[11]

She then reiterated that "[t]he test for probable cause is not reducible to 'precise definition or quantification.'"[12] Kagan emphasized that the Court's prior decisions "rejected rigid rules, bright-line tests, and mechanistic inquiries" in favor of their practical and commonsensical standard based on the totality of the circumstances.[13]

In rejecting the Florida Supreme Court's decision, the U.S. Supreme Court pointed out that its Florida counterpart had "flouted this established approach to determining probable cause. To assess the reliability of a drug-detection dog, the Florida court [had] created a strict evidentiary checklist, whose every item the State [would have to] tick off."[14] Based on this approach, the Court wondered how a "rookie dog" ever could satisfy the state court's test because the absence of any field performance records inevitably would preclude a finding of probable cause.

Based on the U.S. Supreme Court approach, "a probable-cause hearing focusing on a dog's alert should proceed much like any other. The court should allow the parties to make their best case, consistent with the rules of criminal procedure. And, the court then should evaluate the proffered evidence to decide what all the circumstances demonstrate. In all events, the court should not prescribe, as the Florida Supreme Court did, an inflexible set of evidentiary requirements. The question—similar to every inquiry into probable cause—is whether all the facts surrounding a dog's alert, viewed through the lens of common sense, would make a reasonably prudent person think that a search would reveal contraband or evidence of a crime."[15] Based on this approach, Justice Kagan concluded that "[a][dog] sniff is up to snuff when it meets that test" and that in this case Aldo's had.[16]

### FLORIDA V. JARDINES

The more closely watched of the two dog-sniff cases examined by the U.S. Supreme Court during the 2012 term was decided on March 26, 2013. In *Florida v. Jardines,* the Court addressed whether "using a drug-sniffing dog on a homeowner's porch to investigate the contents of the home is a 'search' within the meaning of the Fourth Amendment."[17]

A short recitation of the facts leading up to the legal dispute is important for law enforcement officers who handle drug-sniffing canines. When a detective with the Miami-Dade, Florida, Police Department received an unverified tip that Joelis Jardines was growing marijuana in his home, the department teamed with DEA to investigate.

A surveillance team observed Jardines' home and noted no activity; however, the group could not see inside the residence. A trained canine handler and his drug-sniffing dog (trained to detect marijuana, cocaine, heroin, and several other drugs) approached Jardines' front porch. While doing so the dog sensed one of the odors he had been trained to detect and began "energetically exploring the area for the strongest point source for that odor."[18] After his exploring, the dog sat down at the base of the front door, indicating it as the strongest source. The dog was on a 6-foot leash during this entire incident. The handler and canine then left the scene after the handler informed the investigating detective of the positive alert.

Based mainly on the positive alert to the presence of narcotics, the detective obtained a search warrant and executed it at Jardines' residence later that same day. The search resulted in the seizure of marijuana plants, and Jardines was charged with trafficking in cannabis. Jardines successfully had the evidence suppressed by the trial court on the basis that the canine investigation was an unreasonable search.

After an appellate court reversed the suppression, the Florida Supreme Court reinstated the order to suppress. The state high court "h[eld] (as relevant here) that the use of the trained narcotics dog to investigate Jardines' home was a Fourth Amendment search unsupported by probable cause, rendering invalid the warrant based upon information gathered in that search."[19]

Before examining its decision, it is important to note that the U.S. Supreme Court limited its review of the case to the question of whether the handler and the dog approaching and being on the front porch to detect drug odors constituted a Fourth Amendment search. It is settled that the action of a dog sniffing certain odors in a place where the animal has a legal right to be does not constitute a search.[20] And, of course, the Court dealt with the issue of probable cause being satisfied from a positive alert by a trained dog earlier in the *Harris* case discussed at length in this article.

The U.S. Supreme Court began its analysis of the issue with the following reminder: "The Fourth Amendment provides in relevant part that the 'right of the people to be secure in their persons, houses, papers, and effects, against unreasonable searches and seizures, shall not be violated.' The Amendment establishes a simple baseline, one that for much of our history formed the exclusive basis for its protections: When 'the government obtains information by physically intruding on persons, houses, papers, or effects,' a "search"' within the original meaning of the Fourth Amendment' has 'undoubtedly occurred.'"21 This rather simple formula for determining whether a search took place had been resurrected by the Court in *United States v. Jones* just 1 year before *Jardines*. 22

While the *Jones* case involved government agents placing a tracking device on a vehicle operated by the subject of a drug investigation, *Jardines* involved a subject's *home*—the item at the Fourth Amendment's "very core" and "first among equals" when it comes to the Amendment's protected areas.23 The fact that the investigation actually involved the area "immediately surrounding and associated with the home," or the curtilage, does not change this high level of protection because curtilage is considered "part of the home itself for Fourth Amendment purposes."24 Because it was clear that the officers involved in the investigation in *Jardines* entered his curtilage—the front porch being the "classic exemplar" of such—the Court quickly turned to the "question whether it was accomplished through an unlicensed physical intrusion."25 As physical intrusion in the case was obvious—"it is undisputed that the detectives had all four of their feet and all four of their companion's planted on the constitutionally protected extension of Jardines' home," this issue ultimately boiled down to whether the intrusion was licensed or not.26

Turning first to what homeowners typically invite people (including "solicitors, hawkers, and peddlers of all kinds") to do, the Court noted that there typically is an "implicit license [that] permits [a] visitor to approach the home by the front path, knock promptly, wait briefly to be received, and then (absent invitation to linger longer) leave."[27] Writing for a slim majority of five justices, Justice Antonin Scalia even pointed out that Girl Scouts and trick-or-treaters abide by this traditional invitation routinely. Scalia then concluded that "a police officer not armed with a warrant" could do the same as that is "no more than any private citizen might do."[28] However, that is not what happened in the present case.

The introduction of the trained canine and the explicit quest to uncover contraband and evidence changed this from a situation involving a routine invitee to a much more invasive governmental action. The Court contrasted finding "a visitor knocking on the door" with finding "that same visitor exploring the front path with a metal detector or marching his bloodhound into the garden before saying hello and asking permission." While the former would be invited, the latter would be highly unwelcomed. In fact, it "would inspire most [people] to—well, call the police," the Court noted.[29] While the express or implied license of most homeowners allows people (including law enforcement officers) to enter their porch to knock on their door and briefly wait for a response, the scope of that license is limited and does not allow anyone to linger on that same porch with a trained dog.

Because the Court relied on its rationale articulated in last year's *Jones* decision,[30] it did not have to address the well-known *Katz v. United States*[31] "reasonable expectation of privacy" formulation to determine whether a search had occurred in *Jardines*.[32] In fact, the Court acknowledged that whether the activity involved here did or did not amount to a *Katz*-type search was irrelevant precisely because the *Katz* test "has been *added to,* not *substituted for*" the traditional property-based search test recognized again in *Jones.*[33]

Justice Scalia pointed out that "[o]ne virtue of the Fourth Amendment's property-rights baseline is that it keeps easy cases easy. [Because] officers learned what they learned only by physically intruding on Jardines' property to gather evidence, [that was] enough to establish that a search occurred."[34]

CONCLUSION

Law enforcement officers appreciate easy-to-apply legal principles. Both dog-sniff cases discussed herein set forth straightforward guidance for canine handlers. As Justice Scalia noted in his majority opinion in *Jardines,* applying the Court's Fourth Amendment property-rights search test is easy when a drug-sniffing canine is brought onto a homeowner's curtilage. The U.S. Supreme Court also affirmed a fairly straightforward, common-sense-type test for determining probable cause in its *Harris* drug-sniffing dog case.

The principles on which these cases were decided are at the very core of the Fourth Amendment—that is, how to determine whether "probable cause" exists and whether a "search" has occurred. Together, these two Florida-generated cases involving law enforcement's use of drug dogs have given law enforcement officers solid guidance on determining whether they have probable cause and whether their actions will constitute a search for Fourth Amendment purposes. Law enforcement officers will be able to put these principles to use in their daily activities—not just when using canines but in a whole host of other law enforcement activities, as well.

## ENDNOTES

1 Michael Doyle, "Drug-Sniffing Cases Send Supreme Court to the Dogs," *The Miami Herald,* October 26, 2012, *http://www.miamiherald.com/2012/10/26/3068148/drug-sniffing-cases-send-supreme.html;* and Dana Milbank, "The Supreme Court's Dog-Day Afternoon," *The Washington Post,* October 31, 2012, *http://articles.washingtonpost.com/2012-10-31/opinions/35500075_1_police-dog-justice-elena-kagan-chief-justice.*

2 568 U.S. ___ (2013).

3 U.S. Const. amend. IV provides that "The right of the people to be secure in their persons, houses, papers, and effects against unreasonable searches and seizures shall not be violated, and no Warrants shall issue but upon probable cause, supported by Oath or affirmation, and particularly describing the place to be searched and the persons or things to be seized." The U.S. Supreme Court has concluded that this language dictates that searches conducted without a warrant are per se unreasonable, subject to limited and delineated exceptions. These exceptions include motor vehicle searches (*Carroll v. United States,* 267 U.S. 132 (1925)) when there is probable cause to believe evidence is contained in a motor vehicle.

4 *Supra* note 2, at ___, slip op. at 2.

5 *Id.*

6 *Id.* at ___, slip op. at 3.

7 *Florida v. Harris,* 71 So. 3d 756, 767 (Fla. 2011).

8 *Id.* at 775.

9 *Id.* at 769; and *Id.* at 769, 774.

10 *Supra* note 2, at ___, slip op. at 4, quoting *Florida v. Harris,* n. 7 at 773.

11 *Supra* note 2, at ___, slip op. at 5 (internal quotations omitted).

12 *Id.* at ___, slip op. at 5 (quoting, *Maryland v. Pringle,* 540 U.S. 366, 371 (2003)).

13 *Supra* note 2, at ___, slip op. at 5; and *Supra* note 13, also citing *Illinois v. Gates,* 462 U.S. 213, 232 (1983).

14 *Supra* note 2 at ___, slip op. at 5-6.

15 *Supra* note 2 at ___, slip op. at 9.

16 *Id.*

17 569 U.S. ___, (2013); and 569 U.S. at ___, slip op. at 1.

18 *Id.* at ___, slip op. at 2.

[19] *Id.* at ___, slip op. at 3 (parenthetical in original), citing *Florida v. Jardines,* 73 So. 3d 34 (2011).

[20] *United States v. Place,* 462 U.S. 696 (1983); *Illinois v. Caballes,* 543 U.S. 405 (2005).

[21] *Id.* at ___, slip op. at 3 (quoting *U.S. v. Jones,* 565 U.S. ___, ___ n.3 (2012)) (slip op., at 6, n. 3.).

[22] *U.S. v. Jones,* 565 U.S. ___ (2012).

[23] *Supra* note 19 at ___, slip op. at 4.

[24] *Id.* (quoting *Oliver v. United States,* 466 U.S. 170, 180 (1984)).

[25] *Supra* note 16 at ___, slip op. at 5. In fn. 1 the Court points out that "[a]t oral argument, the State and its *amicus* the solicitor general argued that Jardines conceded in the lower courts that the officers had a right to be where they were. This misstates the record. Jardines conceded nothing more than the unsurprising proposition that the officers could have lawfully approached his home to knock on the front door in hopes of speaking with him. Of course, that is not what they did."

[26] *Supra* note 19 at ___, slip op. at 6.

[27] *Id.*

[28] *Supra* note 19 at ___, slip op. at 6-7 (quoting *Kentucky v. King,* 563 U.S. ___, ___ (2011) (slip op., at 16)).

[29] *Supra* note 19 at ___, slip op. at 7.

[30] *Supra* note 25.

[31] 389 U.S. 347 (1967).

[32] It should be noted, however, that in a concurring opinion written by Justice Kagan and with whom Justices Ginsburg and Sotomayor joined, Justice Kagan concluded that the activity in this case also would have satisfied the *Katz* "reasonable expectation of privacy" definition of a Fourth Amendment search. On the other hand, Justice Alito, in his dissenting opinion joined by Chief Justice Roberts and Justices Kennedy and Breyer, determined that the activity in this case would not have satisfied the *Katz* "reasonable expectation of privacy" definition and, therefore, did not constitute a *Katz*-type search. Justice Alito also opined that the activity did not constitute a trespass and, therefore, was not a search under either search theory.

[33] *Supra* note 19 at ___, slip op. at 9 (quoting *United States v. Jones.)*

565 U.S. \_\_\_, \_\_\_, slip op. at 8 (2012) (emphasis in original)).
[34] Supra note 19 at \_\_\_, slip op. at 9

---

## Discussion Questions

Dog sniff cases are very interesting. Some states, under their constitutions or statutory laws, require search warrants before drug detection dogs can be used on people or vehicles located in public places. Although such activities do not constitute "searches" within the meaning of the Fourth Amendment, these states provide additional protections, which can be viewed as ensuring a higher degree of privacy for its citizens on the one hand, and sheltering criminals and harming law-abiding citizens, on the other. One might even make the argument that by doing so, states deprive crime victims of their rights of equal protection under the Fourteenth Amendment.

*What are your views on this issue?*

# THE DISEASE OF CERTAINTY
By Everett Doolittle, D.P.A.

March 2012: *FBI Law Enforcement Bulletin*

I HAVE HAD GREAT OPPORTUNITIES OVER MY MANY YEARS in law enforcement. I have served as a police officer, a deputy sheriff, and even the chief deputy, but I found my greatest career opportunity at the Minnesota Bureau of Criminal Apprehension (BCA). At BCA, I tackled my most challenging assignment when I led the Cold Case Unit (CCU).

Early in my career, I gained valuable experience by working on homicide teams. But, studying the errors of others and reworking an old case granted me even greater insight into why cases fail. This article describes one of the major sources of these investigative errors: a phenomenon I dubbed the "Disease of Certainty."

The Disease of Certainty is fatal to investigations. Both inexperienced and seasoned officers can catch this contagious disease, and it can spread throughout a team. It occurs when officers feel so convinced of their own beliefs that they allow themselves to become tunnel-visioned about one conclusion and ignore clues that might point them in another direction. Those who resist the disease may be ridiculed and ostracized for their supposed lack of understanding and inability to see the truth if all of their coworkers share the same beliefs and assumptions about the investigation.

The numerous cases that CCU worked over the years taught us many lessons about the Disease of Certainty. For clarification, when I refer to the BCA CCU, I include all members of the BCA team (agents, analysts, forensic scientists, and support personnel) and the local and county investigators who assist these investigations. Cold case investigations demand a multiagency approach to solve a difficult problem, so a diverse set of personnel with varying expertise comprise the team.

By describing what I have learned about the Disease of Certainty, I do not aim to demean the work of the initial agencies involved, but to help others avoid the same mistakes in the future. I want to eliminate this deadly disease of perception that can prevent investigators from seeing beyond their own assumptions. All of these cases involved dedicated and professional individuals, but fatal errors occurred nonetheless. CCU does not aim to judge the initial investigators but to work with the agency as a team to reinvigorate the investigation. One person or agency never deserves all of the credit for cracking a case because it demands a true team effort.

A CASE STUDY

My work with CCU began with numerous rape and assault cases, but I will focus on a series of homicides. The first of the confirmed homicides occurred in December 1978. As the Huling family slept in their secluded rural farm house north of the Twin Cities (St. Paul and Minneapolis) in Minnesota, an intruder entered their home. Before leaving, the intruder viciously murdered Alice Huling and three of her children—miraculously, one survived.

Several other seemingly unrelated crimes occurred over the following year. The next one took place in May 1979 when Marlys Wohlenhaus came home from school. A few hours later, her mother returned from errands and found Marlys severely beaten and unconscious. The girl was pronounced dead 2 days later. Next, in the following months, a young woman disappeared after leaving a restaurant. Though her car quickly was discovered near the Mississippi River, her body was not found for another 5 years. Yet again, soon after, a young girl left another restaurant where witnesses saw her forced into a vehicle, and her body was found days later.

These cases shocked the surrounding communities. However, because no apparent relationship existed between the crimes, the police departments investigated them individually. Several independent investigations continued for many years. In each of the cases, police identified a different prime suspect who became the central focus of the investigation.

## THE DISEASE DEFINED

To understand the seriousness of this issue, I need to explain the investigative process and how problems can arise. There are two logical approaches to problem solving that investigators must understand and use effectively: deductive and inductive reasoning. Deductive reasoning results from the evidence that people see in murder-mystery movies—the smoking gun, witnesses, DNA, fingerprints, and other tangible facts and clues. With deductive reasoning, this evidence builds the foundation of the case, and everything comes together to point to one conclusion.

Unfortunately, most real-life investigations differ greatly from the ones seen on television. In many cases, investigators can gather little if any tangible facts or evidence, which leads to a difficult, complex investigation that quickly can become a cold case. In these instances, investigators must turn to inductive reasoning to evaluate possible directions and outcomes.

Through inductive reasoning, or scenario-based logic, we determine possibilities and probabilities based on experience and intuition and then attempt to prove or disprove them. Investigators start with a simple question, for example: Who killed Marlys Wohlenhaus? Could it be her boyfriend? What would be his motive? Could it be her stepfather or the neighbor kid who lives down the block? What would be their motives? Investigators attempt to identify possibilities and eliminate them one by one until only the most probable solution remains. To the seasoned investigator, this type of reasoning becomes the routine course of action.

These types of reasoning can go awry when in the mind of an investigator a possibility becomes the only reality. When officers become convinced of a certain solution, they may think that others who disagree with their answer simply do not understand. In most cases, experienced investigators' instincts are correct, and their prime suspect indeed committed the crime. Nevertheless, one always must keep an open mind to the facts that disagree with an initial assessment as probability does not equate to certainty. Anyone can come to an incorrect first conclusion, especially when little or no straightforward evidence exists, and a conclusion is based mainly on conjecture.

## THE CASE RESOLVED

In the serial murders outlined above, this Disease of Certainty led law enforcement personnel to disregard key information because it did not agree with their previous conclusions. However, when CCU reopened the case, many new hypotheses developed, and answers were found among the volumes of information the initial investigators had gathered. As in many cold cases, this only could happen when some initial investigators were removed and new personnel were assigned to support the case.

Eventually, CCU solved these crimes by examining a suspect who quickly had been cleared in the initial investigation. This man was not an acquaintance, stepfather, priest, or deputy, but a stranger. Joseph Ture was a drifter who lived in his car at a rest stop about 4 miles from the Huling home. Four days after the murders, police arrested Ture for an unrelated crime and found a ski mask, a club wrapped in leather, and a small toy car in his possession. These items became significant years later.

Two years later, in 1981, Ture was arrested and convicted of the murder of another waitress. While awaiting trial, he supposedly talked to his cellmate about his involvement in the murders of the Huling family and Marlys Wohlenhaus, and his statements were forwarded to law enforcement agencies. When officers questioned Ture, he maintained his innocence and claimed he was working at an automobile plant in St. Paul when the homicides occurred. The investigators contacted the plant and confirmed that a Joseph Ture was working on the assembly line at the time of the murder of Marlys Wohlenhaus. As a result, the officers eliminated Ture as a suspect.

When CCU personnel examined this case 20 years later, however, they reconsidered evidence, such as

Ture's statements to his cellmate and the items he possessed at the time of his initial arrest. They double-checked Ture's alibi and realized that it actually was Joseph Ture, Sr., the suspect's father, who worked at the automobile plant at the time of the murder. Upon further inquiry, CCU members discovered other incriminating remarks that the suspect made to his cellmate. Ture divulged information that only someone with direct involvement in the crime would have known. Also, the team found that Billy Huling, the one surviving child of the Huling home, could identify the toy car found with Ture when he was arrested decades earlier; Billy and his brother, Wayne, had played with a similar one prior to the night their family was murdered.

This example illustrates how investigators can become too convinced of their own conclusions. Because Joseph Ture allegedly was working at the time of the Wohlenhaus murder, officers disregarded other significant evidence against him. Once CCU reexamined previously held truths about the case (such as Ture's alibi), they solved the crimes. This case has appeared numerous times on television.

### Dangers of Overconfidence

Over the years, I have seen priests, deputy sheriffs, stepfathers, neighborhood kids, boyfriends, parents, spouses, and other innocent suspects become not only the focus of the investigation but the only possible answer in the minds of investigators. Once investigators develop this mind-set, it takes courage for others to stand up and disagree with the one perceived truth.

Also, this Disease of Certainty seriously can damage innocent individuals who mistakenly become the focus of the investigation. In some instances, little or no factual evidence exists against a suspect, yet the police, community, and media all believe the individual committed the crime. Rather than grieving the loss of a friend, acquaintance, or loved one, the suspect must deal with being viewed as a criminal in the eyes of the public.

Investigators face the challenge of pursuing their work confidently and proactively, yet understanding that they can be wrong and that if they are their errors impact many people. In this way, officers hold much power and influence over the lives of others, and their ethics matter a great deal. Police may want to solve cases quickly by relying on their instincts and investigating aggressively, but they also have a duty to remain open-minded, fair, and thorough. Working cold cases, I have seen the conflicts that arise when these priorities fall out of balance.

CCU's success in identifying Ture as the murderer in no way detracts from the competency of the original investigators. But, to combat the Disease of Certainty, agencies must remember that personnel assigned to a particular case do not "own" that investigation. In the serial murders described above, the initial investigative teams included experienced officers who had long records of success, yet their experience may have contributed to their failures. These errors, while understandable, may not have occurred had the investigators not formed such strong beliefs of who committed the crimes. Experienced investigators draw on their past successes, which may blind them to unexpected possibilities.

## A WIDE PERSPECTIVE

Many of the cases worked by CCU, like the Wohlenhaus and Huling murders, involved talented and dedicated personnel who focused too narrowly on one hypothetical conclusion. One incorrect hypothesis should not jeopardize an entire case. Every investigation reveals several paths that can lead in any number of directions, and, if it dead-ends, investigators need to turn around and try a new one. Problems arise, however, when police venture down the wrong path and refuse to see that they are going in the wrong direction.

Once investigators develop this fixed mind-set, they filter out information that disagrees with their conclusion and only see the evidence that supports their answers. I have observed this phenomenon often while managing multiagency task forces and referred to it as the "Don Quixote Effect." Don Quixote, a famous literary hero, mistakenly battled windmills because he believed so strongly that they were giants. This idea resonates in Thomas Kuhn's 1962 book, The Structure of Scientific Revolutions, which discusses the difficulties experienced by scientists when they discovered information that disagreed with their long-held truths or paradigms.

Overconfidence is not the only way that the Disease of Certainty can infiltrate an investigation. Sometimes, a lack of perspective leads the team awry. When investigators dig deeply into the facts of a case, they can become too focused on one suspect, one lead, or one piece of information and lose sight of the bigger picture. This line of thinking caused investigators to mistakenly eliminate Joseph Ture as a suspect in the crimes described above.

When venturing into a densely wooded forest—it is easy to lose sight of the forest when surrounded by trees. Similarly, when officers become bogged down by puzzling information and unanswered questions, they may find it difficult to see the bigger picture of the case. Solving a difficult and complex investigation with keen inductive reasoning demands more than a team of dedicated personnel; it requires a leader. True leaders can see beyond disparate facts and seemingly unrelated evidence to view the whole "forest," and they have the courage to tell others when they are heading in the wrong direction.

## CONCLUSION

Because the Cold Case Unit receives cases after a significant amount of time has passed and all initial leads have been exhausted, it brings a fresh perspective to the puzzle. CCU's investigators are not the same team of officers who responded to the scene of the crime, interviewed witnesses, interacted with a grieving family, and felt the pressure of media attention that surrounds high-profile cases; because of this, they may provide a new approach missing from the initial investigation.

Additionally, because CCU receives cases that stumped a dedicated team of investigators, cold case officers know they must consider "out-of-the-box" solutions and, thus, are less susceptible to the Disease of Certainty. A unit, such as ours at BCA, can provide this service for any agency willing to challenge experienced investigators' long-held beliefs and dig into old cases. Agencies must remember that even their most talented officers can fall victim to overconfidence, and this Disease of Certainty may have caused errors in cold cases that still can be resolved.

---

### DISCUSSION QUESTION

Hungarian Scientist Albert Szent-Gyorgyi said, "Discovery consists of seeing what everyone has seen and thinking what nobody has thought." How do you think such a statement fits with the "Disease of Certainty"?

## CRITICAL THINKING EXERCISE

The author of this article makes a very good point regarding the scientific investigative process, but there is much more to this than deductive and inductive reasoning. As a group, develop a short outline on the process to include how hypotheses are formed, and how inductive and deductive reasoning can be incorporated into the process. Be sure to provide short definitions of the terms that you use and how they apply to a criminal investigation.

# Child Fatality Review Boards
By
Gerald Kelley

March 2010: *FBI Law Enforcement Bulletin*

*A statue stands in a shaded place,*
*An angel girl with an upturned face,*
*A name is written on a polished rock,*
*A broken heart that the world forgot.*[1]

IN 1987, THE DEATH OF A 7-YEAR-OLD BOY AT THE HAND OF his mother's live-in boyfriend raised many questions about the procedures and practices used by the area's agencies that protected and served children. Newspaper articles brought into question the roles and responsibilities of the various organizations that had dealt with the family prior to the youngster's death and why a closer working relationship did not exist among them. These questions were directed at the local children's social service, the schools, and the police because all had contact with the family. But, the information that each possessed was either not available or only so in small amounts to the other agencies involved. What could the community do to ensure better coordination among these entities? To illustrate an effective solution, the author presents an overview of the child fatality review process by using an example from his local community of Summit County, Ohio.

## DEVELOPING THE PLAN

Following the tragic death of the young boy, the children's services board initiated an effort to address the communication problem among the community's agencies. Members brought in experts from the medical, social, and legal fields for a symposium that presented information on how other communities had banded together to review child fatalities and seek preventive solutions. Relying on models in practice, a core group of participants gathered to study and begin the review process of child fatalities. The committee, composed of representatives from local child-serving agencies, public health officials, medical practitioners, the medical examiner, prosecutors, and law enforcement personnel, began with two main goals.

- To review all child deaths and near deaths due to child abuse and neglect, to assess each involved-agency's system performance, to make recommendations for the improvement of intra- and interagency performance, and to reduce the number of preventable deaths in the county

- To present to the community a statement of the committee's analysis and findings

The committee relied on child fatality review models established in other communities, particularly the one in Los Angeles, California, that focused on a multiagency approach to coordinate the information each organization possessed. This approach enabled individual agencies to benefit from the exchange of information and improve performance as related to the welfare of children.[2] Since its beginning in 1978, the child fatality review process now exists in all 50 states and has expanded from a core membership to include representatives from education, other health-related agencies, and the courts, along with prosecutors and other professionals as deemed necessary. It also now encompasses not only deaths from abuse and neglect but also those as a result of natural causes, accidents, and suicides.

In July 2000, Ohio passed a law mandating that each county in the state establish a child fatality review board governed by its department of health. To accomplish the law's ultimate purpose of reducing the incidence of preventable child deaths,[3] each review board would:

- promote cooperation, collaboration, and communication among all groups that serve families and children;
- maintain a database of all child deaths to develop an understanding of the causes and incidences of them; and
- recommend and develop plans for implementing local service and program changes and advise the department of health of aggregated data, trends, and patterns found in child deaths.[4]

### IMPLEMENTING THE PROCESS

The Summit County Child Fatality Review Board examines all of the child deaths that have occurred within the jurisdiction and incidents involving youngsters who lived in the county but died outside the area. The process starts with each member receiving a packet provided by the county's department of health that includes the death and birth certificates for each child who recently died except those involved in a pending criminal investigation.[5] As with all cases reviewed, confidentiality is required by law.

First, the board examines the death certificate, which provides the cause and manner of death as determined by the medical examiner or the child's physician when the case does not involve the medical examiner. Next, it reviews the birth certificate, which covers general information about the child and the parents and details regarding the mother's pregnancy history, both past and current.

In reviewing cases involving abuse or neglect, the committee members report on the contact they have had with the family. Children's social services will provide a history of their investigations regarding any abuse and neglect and their referrals to other agencies for follow-up assistance or training. This could range from life-skills training to medical services. Health providers will discuss training and other assistance provided to the family, for example, referrals that the parents received during and after the child's birth to the Help Me Grow program.[6] With older children, the schools can provide information on their progress and whether they have had disciplinary or attendance issues.

Both areas can be indicators of problems occurring within the family. Once again, where concern for a child has arisen, each agency will show what steps it has taken to correct the problem or to refer family members to another organization better suited to help them. Law enforcement will discuss contacts with the youngster and the family regarding arrests, calls of service to the household, and missing person reports about the child. While arrests are important factors to consider, they do not always reflect the complete dynamics of the family. Calls of service can reveal incidents of domestic violence and other family-related difficulties where no arrest took place. Missing person reports also can prove significant because many involve a juvenile running from a situation.

Combining all of the information from the reporting agencies creates a clearer picture of the child's life and the roles that the community's various agencies have played in it. The information also can show the deficiencies, or "holes," in the system that needs correction.

After presenting all of the information, the committee discusses whether the death could have been prevented. Was a known safety risk ignored, or was the family even aware of the risk due to a lack of information? However, not all of the public information regarding safe practices is consistent.

| Websites for Additional Information | |
|---|---|
| American Academy of Pediatrics | *http://www.aap.org* |
| Centers for Disease Control and Prevention | *http://www.cdc.gov* |
| Inter-Agency Council on Child Abuse and Neglect | *http://ican.co.la.ca.us/home.htm* |
| National Center on Child Fatality Review | *http://ican-ncfr.org* |
| SIDS Network | *http://sids-network.org* |

For example, some private organizations encourage sleeping with a newborn to promote bonding between the parents and the child. However, this practice can prove deadly if a parent rolls over on top of the child while sleeping. Each year, the committee investigates and reviews cases that list this as either the cause of or as a contributing factor to an infant's death. Some of these deaths are ruled undetermined if the medical examiner cannot ascertain whether they resulted from asphyxiation or a criminal act.

During this portion of the process, committee members often discover additional information that may have contributed to the death. For example, during a discussion about an infant who died in a crib, a member asked about the make and model of the bed. It turned out that the manufacturer had recalled the crib for structural problems. Another member then suggested that the committee notify all of the community's social service agencies about the recall and have them check the model against any donated cribs that they had received. Members compiled a list of organizations and sent out an informational letter describing the committee's safety concerns with the recalled crib and the potential dangers of its continued use.

## USING THE INFORMATION

Local child fatality review boards analyze the data they have collected for trends occurring in their counties. They address the necessary means and modes to educate the community to eliminate preventable deaths. Programs have mirrored national campaigns, such as the Back to Sleep and Don't Shake programs.[7] Members gather resources for educational purposes and distribute them throughout the community. In certain instances, as with the Don't Shake program, volunteers provide personal instruction to schools and other groups. With most review committees relying on their agency members for operating costs, they have to be extremely resourceful to get their message out. They have turned to their communities and local member agencies to provide funding for informational flyers, training videos, and other aids, which they distribute to schools, social programs, health departments, hospitals, private doctors, and retail businesses.

Each county review board sends the data it has collected to the state's department of health where such information forms the basis for the state's annual report of child deaths. The boards include their decisions concerning whether they believed that any deaths could have been prevented. These are subjective decisions based upon their reviews, which rely heavily on information gathered from investigations of the deaths and medical records of the deceased children.

To aid their local child fatality review committees, law enforcement personnel and medical examiners must conduct thorough investigations of all deaths. Scene investigations are essential to the successful completion of all cases, both criminal and noncriminal. This proves especially important when investigating the death of a child. Many community organizations use the observations and information gathered from the scene to better understand why the child died and to determine if the death could have been prevented. Concise documentation of seemingly unimportant details, including sleeping conditions and positions, the victim's clothing, and room temperature, can provide the clues necessary for an accurate ruling on the death. All of this information then becomes part of the department of health's statistics. The more accurate the investigations, the better the analysis of why children die, which may lead to the development of ways to prevent such tragedies.

## CONCLUSION

Child fatality review boards have been in existence for only 30 years. Since their inception, they have expanded both geographically and in content. From analyzing child abuse and neglect cases to studying all child deaths, their ultimate goal is the prevention of these tragic occurrences. Studies have shown that projects like the Back to Sleep program have reduced the number of sudden deaths of infants by as much as 40 percent.[8] Law enforcement has a major role to play in this process by conducting thorough scene investigations. This information, along with data obtained from medical examiner autopsies, will present an accurate picture of the manner of death. With this valuable information, the development of prevention programs can be directed toward reversing these fatalities.

ENDNOTES

[1] Martina McBride, "Concrete Angel," *Greatest Hits*, RCA Records, 2001, written by Stephanie Bentley and Rob Crosby, produced by Martina McBride and Paul Worley.

[2] Michael Durfee, George Gellert, and Deanne Tilton-Durfee, "Origins and Clinical Relevance of Child Death Review Teams," *Journal of the American Medical Association* 267 (1992): 3172-3175.

[3] See Ohio Department of Health, Child Fatality Review website at *http://www.odh.ohio.gov/odhPrograms/cfhs/cfr/cfr1.aspx*.

[4] Counties that had review committees converted them to follow the guidelines established by the state's new law. These deaths are either briefly reviewed or postponed until the prosecution is completed or the case has been closed by law enforcement.

[6] For information on this program, access *http://www.ohiohelpmegrow.org*.

[7] For information on the Back to Sleep program, access *http://www.nichd.nih.gov/sids/* and for the Don't Shake program, access *http://www.dontshakejake.org/*.

[8] See Ohio Department of Health, Sudden Infant Death website at *http://www.odh.ohio.gov/odhPrograms/cfhs/sid/sids1.aspx*.

## Critical Thinking Exercise

Undertake research in your jurisdiction (county or state) to see if a Child Fatality Review Board or similar organization exists. Attempt to ascertain whether the review team has identified any anomalies or inconsistencies in the cause and manner of deaths.

# FALSE ALLEGATIONS OF ADULT CRIMES
By James McNamara, M.S., and
Jennifer Lawrence, M.A.

September 2012: *FBI Law Enforcement Bulletin*

A T 7:30 A.M., AN UNKNOWN MALE ABDUCTED PAMELA AT knifepoint while she fueled her car at a convenience store. The offender then forced her to drive to a bridge, where they crossed into a neighboring state. During the long ride, he choked her with a bicycle security chain and slashed her with a knife.

Next, the assailant ordered Pamela to park the vehicle in a secluded rural area and led her into the woods. He bound her to a tree, placing the bicycle chain around her neck. The subject then assaulted her vaginally with a box cutter and lacerated her breasts and right nipple.

Then, he ordered Pamela back into her car and had her drive them to a nearby ferry. The subject exited the vehicle and disappeared while heading toward the ferry at about 3 p.m. Pamela drove herself to the nearest hospital for treatment, and staff members notified the police. After receiving medical attention, she was released.

State and local police investigators conducted the initial interview of Pamela at the hospital. Although initially cooperative, she stopped answering questions. Pamela agreed to meet investigators at a later date at the state police barracks to discuss the abduction and sexual assault, but she never arrived.

A review of hospital medical records showed that Pamela received treatment for superficial lacerations to her right hand, left breast, right breast and nipple, and neck. She also had several superficial abrasions in her pubic region. The doctor described her as tired but in no acute discomfort.

Officers found no forensic evidence from Pamela or her vehicle. They contacted the FBI's National Center for the Analysis of Violent Crime (NCAVC) for assistance in developing an interview strategy. Investigators determined that Pamela suffered from depression and anxiety and had a prescription for an antidepressant. Working with NCAVC, officers developed a successful interview strategy, and Pamela finally admitted that she fabricated the abduction and sexual assault.

Her false allegation tied up the resources of several state and local police departments, as well as the area FBI office. Significant media attention focused on the case prior to her confession. An artist's sketch of the imaginary offender circulated. The media quoted a spokesperson for a local women's rape crisis center as saying, "What I see is a community that is scared...."

BACKGROUND

A false allegation crime involves persons reporting a fabricated offense that has occurred against them to a law enforcement agency. Both men and women commit these crimes; however, women perpetrate the majority of them. A limited number of studies have focused on false allegation adult crimes, with the majority of research addressing cases of rape and to a lesser degree stalking.[1]

These offenses occur throughout America every year. Unfortunately, they waste substantial investigative resources—needed for legitimate cases involving real victims—before authorities can identify them as false allegations. And, as noted in the quote from the crisis center worker, these false allegations can severely affect communities and the people who live and work there. Worse, they can make it harder for law enforcement agencies and citizens to take real victims of crime seriously.

### OFFENDER MOTIVATIONS

Perpetrators of false allegation crimes have various underlying motivations that fall into one or more categories. Investigators may encounter cases involving more than one motivation.[2]

- Mental illness/depression
- Attention/sympathy
- Financial/profit
- Alibi
- Revenge

A significant life problem (e.g., marital, financial, employment) that the offender does not have the skills to resolve drives the motivation. Many perpetrators have multiple life difficulties. Rather than seeking appropriate assistance from family members, coworkers, clergy members, or mental health professionals, offenders develop a self-victimization plan. These individuals may realize temporary relief from their life problems due to immediate attention and support from family, neighbors, and coworkers. And, more often than not, false allegation offenders do not consider the serious, long-term law enforcement investigation or significant media coverage that reveals the truth. In the long run, offenders are worse off than before the false allegation crime report and even may face prosecution.

Typically, female offenders want to gain attention and sympathy and will falsely allege offenses, such as interpersonal violence (e.g., sexual assault), more likely to achieve that result. While the desire for attention and sympathy also can motivate males, they tend to opt for nonsexual offenses, such as physical assault or attempted murder.[3] Offenders who falsely allege more impersonal crimes, like theft or vandalism, more likely will have financial or profit motives. And, in cases where the perpetrator has no motive or incentive, mental health issues may prove significant.

#### INVESTIGATIONS

Law enforcement officers may find false allegation crimes complex and difficult to unravel. Further, investigators working closely with offenders may become so emotionally invested in the case that they have a hard time believing that the individual could be deceptive.

A suspected false allegation requires a two-pronged approach—covert and overt. Of course, overt investigation proves necessary in the early phase of the case before officers identify the complaint as a false allegation. If the claim is legitimate, investigators need to identify and apprehend the offender. They should use all normal resources and carefully protect the reporting victim's reputation.

The covert investigation focuses on establishing whether the case involves a false allegation crime. Keeping this prong covert helps to avoid prematurely accusing a legitimate victim of a false allegation, prevent derailing the overt investigation, and preserve valuable information for the subject interview. Officers must gather all possible details concerning offenders. Because false allegation perpetrators have serious life problems motivating them, the covert investigation quietly must identify which issues trouble the individual.

This type of information proves crucial during the interview process. Investigators need to examine offenders' personal relationships, employment situation, finances, past criminal history, and other areas of their life to identify any indication of abnormal stress.

Additionally, the covert investigation determines if the offender has made other false allegations or crime reports. Officers also should check with local emergency rescue departments or hospital emergency rooms to discover any false injury or illness reports made by the individual. As the covert investigation progresses, the lead investigator responsible for the overall coordination of the case should receive all information.

The experience of NCAVC and research related to this phenomenon have shown that false allegation adult crimes usually involve only one offender. In most cases, the individual conducts preplanning, preparation, or staging of the crime scene.[4] Fewer incidents of false allegation adult crime arise from spur-of-the-moment decisions. Many cases have involved more than one offense reported simultaneously to law enforcement (e.g., carjacking/extortion, abduction/rape). Investigators need to carefully scrutinize forensic evidence and injuries for inconsistencies.

In collaboration with other law enforcement agencies and academic institutions, the BAUs also conduct research into various crime areas. Additionally, the BAUs share the knowledge gained through operational experience and research with law enforcement agencies through a variety of training venues.

For example, while working the night shift, Charles, an experienced patrol officer for a medium-sized city police department, stopped a vehicle in a deserted area outside of town. Shortly thereafter, he reported that the driver produced a .22 caliber handgun and shot him in the torso at close range. Responding officers could not locate a vehicle or suspect in the area. Further, the bullet hit Charles in an ideal place on his ballistic vest and was deflected, causing him no injury.

Investigators quickly determined that he could not describe his shooter or the vehicle he pulled over. As the investigation progressed, Charles would not give a detailed statement about the incident and declined a polygraph test. The covert investigation in the case uncovered that he faced extreme personal stress due to a problematic marriage and several extramarital affairs.

Investigators eventually gained a confession from Charles and determined that he got the idea from an incident in a neighboring county the night before wherein a deputy sheriff was shot and killed during a traffic stop. Charles staged his own shooting to gain attention and sympathy.

### INTERVIEW STRATEGIES

When allegations prove false, often no forensic evidence exists. Most testimony by eyewitnesses tends to offer exclusively post-offense details and include only information provided by the offender. As a result, the ability of investigators to gain an admission or confession from the perpetrator can become crucial in resolving the case.

Officers face the challenge of determining which life problems have caused the offender to present a false report to law enforcement. Generally, the most effective interviews involve an empathetic approach toward the subject. Directly challenging offenders with inconsistencies in their account or the lack of hard evidence likely will make them shut down or stubbornly insist on the accuracy of their story. After establishing rapport, interviewers need to address the person's life problems. However, empathetic does not mean sympathetic. Authorities can express an understanding of difficulties that caused the situation without condoning the behavior. By addressing the offender's underlying issues, interviewers eliminate the need to argue over the allegation's contradictions or the lack of evidence and more likely will gain a confession.

Katrina was an undergraduate student at a large state university. At the end of a weekend, her roommate returned to their dorm room to find Katrina gone. Her wallet, keys, purse, mobile phone, and laptop all remained in the room. There were no signs of a struggle or forced entry.

The roommate notified local police who began an intensive abduction investigation. However, investigators immediately suspected a false allegation abduction case. They contacted NCAVC for a crime analysis. NCAVC personnel concurred that the case was a false allegation and provided an interview strategy to use when Katrina reappeared.

After a few days, Katrina returned. Interviewers gained a confession from her by using an empathetic approach in an hour-long interview. Beforehand, investigators determined that Katrina felt that her relationship with her boyfriend was at risk and that she desired his attention and sympathy. Further, authorities discovered that she previously made a false report of an assault that proved unfounded (lacking sufficient evidence).

Unfortunately, Katrina's case gained national media attention and caused a major upheaval in and around the university. And, the investigating police department depleted its annual overtime budget searching for her.

## POSSIBLE CLUES

Several indicators can help investigators identify a false allegation case. While none of these signs by themselves indicate a false allegation case, investigators should strongly consider a two-prong investigation with the corroboration of two or more. The offender may:

- continue to make inconsistent statements conflicting prior claims by the individual or information provided by witnesses;
- offer descriptions or circumstances of the reported offense that do not seem plausible or realistic;
- show deception on a polygraph or refuse to take one;
- have a history of mental and emotional problems or false allegations;
- make the allegation after a similar crime received publicity (suggesting modeling or a copycat motive in which the similarity to the publicized crime offers credibility); or
- provide an allegation that lacks substantiating forensic, physical, or medical evidence and does not agree with laboratory findings.

## SOURCE OF ASSISTANCE

The FBI's NCAVC provides advice and assistance in the general areas of crimes against adults, counterterrorism and threat assessment, and crimes against children. Typical cases received for assessment at NCAVC include serial murder, kidnapping, serial sexual assault, stalking, threat assessment, domestic and international terrorism, and false allegation crimes. NCAVC staff members handle requests for assistance from both domestic and international law enforcement agencies.

NCAVC reviews specific crimes from behavioral, forensic, and investigative perspectives. This analytical process serves as a tool for client law enforcement agencies by providing them with an evaluation of the offense, as well as an understanding of the criminal motivations and behavioral characteristics of the offender. Staff members also conduct research in the area of violent crime from a law enforcement perspective to gain insight into criminal thought processes, motivations, and behaviors. NCAVC shares its findings with the law enforcement community through publications, training, and application to the investigative and operational functions of the center.

Personnel typically consult on cases, such as false allegation crimes, when requested by the investigating agency. NCAVC will assist by providing behavioral analysis and investigative and interview strategies. Only law enforcement agencies and prosecutor's offices can receive services from NCAVC.

## Conclusion

Although false allegation adult crimes tend to be the exception, rather than the rule, these cases present serious concerns to law enforcement. Investigators find them difficult and frustrating. Officers risk being accused of not treating crime victims properly by prematurely labeling their allegations as false or by being unable to resolve the case. Further, a tremendous amount of department resources (which could be applied to real victims of real crimes), such as overtime, forensic budgets, and work hours, can be wasted on them.

Realizing how to identify false allegation crimes by using the two-prong investigation and developing the appropriate interview strategy based on the offender's true motivations/life problems allows investigators to more easily and quickly resolve these cases. This will save significant department resources and put the community at ease.

ENDNOTES
[1] K. Mohandie, C. Hatcher, and D. Raymond, "False Victimization Syndromes in Stalking," in *The Psychology of Stalking: Clinical and Forensic Perspectives,* ed. R. Meloy (San Diego, CA: Academic Press, 1998), 225-255.
[2] T.P. Carney, *Practical Investigation of Sex Crimes* (Boca Raton, FL: CAC Press, 2004); and E.J. Kanin, "False Rape Allegations," *Archive of Sexual Behavior* 23, no. 1 (1994): 81-92.
[3] J. McNamara, S. McDonald, and J. Lawrence, "Characteristics of False Allegation Adult Crimes," *Journal of Forensic Science* 57, no. 3 (May 2012): 643-646.
[4] Ibid.; and J.M. Taupin, "Clothing Damage Analysis and the Phenomenon of the False Sexual Assault," *Journal of Forensic Science* 45, no. 3 (2000): 568-572.

## Discussion Questions

1. What do you believe is the most important investigative strategy in resolving a suspected false allegation made by an adult? Why?

2. Based upon the facts provided in this article involving the "Katrina" case, what do you think of NCAVC's initial conclusion?

## Critical Thinking Exercise

The author provides some excellent examples of "red flags," which suggest the possibility of a false allegation. There are others that are used in the field of criminal investigation. As a team, research and provide in outline form, other red flags related to adult false allegations.

## Prostitution and Human Trafficking: A Paradigm Shift
### By Steve Marcin

### March 2013: *FBI Law Enforcement Bulletin*

IN 2010 THE ANAHEIM POLICE DEPARTMENT (APD) VICE detail in Orange County, California, realized that most of the prostitutes it had contact with came from similar backgrounds. Analysis of their common circumstances and reasons for prostituting caused investigators to believe that they were sex trafficking victims. Human trafficking is using force, fraud, or coercion to recruit, obtain, or provide a person for sexual exploitation. This shift in perspective produced an innovative approach to addressing the problem.

In over 100 arrests, most of the women expressed that prostitution was not their career of choice. In a 1998 study, 88 percent of the prostituted women surveyed stated that they wanted to leave the sex trade industry.[1] The majority of prostitutes interviewed by APD vice investigators believed that selling themselves was their only alternative for survival. Further investigation showed that these women shared similar circumstances that led them to prostitution. Many came from dysfunctional homes, had few friends or family members who cared about them, and were drug addicts or alcoholics. Arrest and contact data indicated that most of these women were between 18 and 29 years old.

Unfortunate situations and poor choices made them vulnerable.

Most of the women described their path into the sex trade as a boyfriend transforming into a pimp or a girlfriend becoming a prostitute. A man recognized the woman's situation and gained access through affection, compassion, and a promise to care. He became a companion who listened, understood, and shared the desire for a better future. The new beau quickly made an offer—leave with him and he would take care of her. She left for a better life.

The man quickly moved her to another county or state. Once relocated, the partnership transitioned into an abusive domestic relationship. The man dominated the woman and controlled where she stayed, when and what she ate, what clothes she wore, what she did, and when she did it. Even if the woman could call for help, she had no one to rescue her. The man told her that they needed money and that she would have to earn it. People see a pimp as someone who obtains customers for a prostitute.

The reality is that they use manipulation, threats, and violence to keep these women from leaving. They depend on the women they recruit into prostitution. These men use mental, emotional, and physical abuse to keep the women generating money.[2] Out of fear or a desire to be cared for, hookers protect their pimps. The men abandon women who are unable or unwilling to provide any more revenue. Most prostitutes recognize their actions as illegal; however, a substantial number of them truly are victims.

Pimps use various control methods to keep the women working the streets. Many of the prostitutes spoke of daily physical abuse, emotional dominance, and lies about caring. These men burned the women with curling irons, strangled, and punched them. They told the prostitutes that their families would be ashamed of them for being a hooker and that no one else would care for them.

Alone and removed from family and friends, these women have no money and depend on their pimps for food, shelter, and clothing. Human sex trafficking victims equate to modern day slaves. The vice detail's findings supported the argument that "The most insidious and common pattern appeared to be young women being convinced to exploit themselves for the financial benefit of someone else. Betrayals by the people closest to prostituted women appeared to be only the first injustice in a path . . . rife with violence, degradation, and extreme physical stress."[3]

After close analysis of prostitutes and their situations, the APD instituted a new approach where it viewed prostitution as possible human trafficking. The recognition, rescue, and aid of these victims became the most important tactic in addressing the problem.

## TRADITIONAL APPROACH

Traditionally, the role of law enforcement agencies is to enforce laws. The response to street prostitution has been to arrest hookers. This approach was narrow in scope and usually did not involve the pimp. The standard procedure was for undercover officers to pose as customers, obtain a solicitation, and arrest the prostitute.

They repeated the process often to incarcerate as many women as possible. These tactics resulted in misdemeanor filings and a temporary relocation of the activity. Prostitution soon returned. This rebound resulted from new prostitutes arriving in the area. The new hookers and pimps had no idea what law enforcement efforts previously took place. The activity gradually increased until the police reacted and conducted another undercover operation. The cycle repeated itself.

## Paradigm Shift

The APD dramatically changed its tactics. The goal became rescuing women from their pimps and redirecting their lives, reducing prostitution one life at a time. This paradigm shift meant considering prostitutes as potential victims and identifying pimps as suspects. This role transition became the basis of a new approach where prostitution activity was viewed as potential human sex trafficking. The department adopted new strategies to—

- assist women in escaping prostitution;
- help them realize their situations and the circumstances that got them there;
- provide services to assist with redirecting their lives in a positive direction; and
- seek cooperation in pursuing the pimps who trafficked them as prostitutes.

The APD implemented this new approach by instituting several tactics.

1. *REMOVE THE PROSTITUTES.* Undercover vice investigators contact street walkers, obtain solicitations, take the women into custody, and transport them to the police department.

2. *BEGIN THE TRANSFORMATION.* At the department, officers remove the handcuffs and direct the women to a special interview room, an office converted to be comfortable. Victim advocates and volunteers decorate the room with soft-colored paint, a couch, love seat, lamps, blankets, magazines, paintings, and stuffed animals.

3. *RESCUE THE VICTIMS.* Arresting officers explain to the women that they rescued them. They discuss the manipulation and control that led the victims into prostitution. This experience becomes emotional once the women realize their situation.

4. *CORRECT THE LIFE COURSE.* The APD collaborates with a nonprofit victim advocacy organization to obtain advocates for the victims. Once the women's mind-set shifts from in-custody prostitute to human trafficking victim, the investigator introduces the practitioner. The officer leaves the room to allow for counseling and assistance. The women receive a change of clothes and a backpack of toiletries, makeup, and other essentials. The advocate offers food, shelter, counseling, transportation, job training, and life-management skills. Occasionally, the women reject this approach and submit to their current situation. Most victims accept this assistance and express their desire for a better life.

5. *COLLECT THE EVIDENCE.* The top priority is to rescue these women and prevent them from returning to prostitution. The second priority is to pursue the trafficker. After the recovery process begins, investigators reintroduce themselves. They seek cooperation in building a case against the pimp. Vice officers gather evidence, including statements, hotel register records, video surveillance tapes, cell phone pictures, and text messages.

6. *PURSUE THE PIMP.* When they obtain sufficient evidence, vice investigators seek out and arrest the pimp. A prostitution arrest results in a misdemeanor citation, with the hooker getting

out of jail and working again within a few hours. If the prostitute remains in custody, the pimp obtains another woman. In California, pimping and pandering charges carry a minimum sentence of 3 years in state prison. Arresting the pimp results in a bigger impact on deterring prostitution activity.

7. *PROSECUTE THE TRAFFICKER.* This human trafficking approach initially surprised the Orange County District Attorney's Office. Pimping and pandering prosecutions were rare, with only three such arrests in Anaheim between 2008 and August 2011, when this program started. Presenting newly-reformed street prostitutes as victims in court brought uncertainty and reluctance from filing deputy district attorneys. The APD vice sergeant and investigators hosted meetings and training sessions with deputy district attorneys to outline the new approach, its impact on prostitution, and the potential to save lives. Prosecutors recognized the jury appeal in presenting the story of human trafficking and equating it to sex slavery. The vice sergeant became a court expert in pimping, pandering, and human trafficking. Successful prosecutions brought confidence and enthusiasm toward Anaheim's human trafficking filings. These cases now have a reputation for quality, thoroughness, and jury appeal.

This project has provided an innovative method to address prostitution. Success stories of women rescued from sex trafficking provide a human measure of this effort. From the project's inception in August 2011 through April 2012, the APD vice detail has saved 29 women from their traffickers. Almost 40 percent are under 18 years old. Of those juveniles, records indicated that 77 percent were missing persons. Traffickers transported 81 percent of the 29 out of their home counties.

## SUCCESS STORIES

Each rescue is significant. The examples provided follow the victims through prosecution of their traffickers. These represent 2 of 29 cases demonstrating how this problem-solving method accomplished more than reducing calls for service.

When the Anaheim vice detail conducted a covert prostitution operation, officers observed Jessica (not her real name) walking the street. An undercover investigator contacted her, obtained a solicitation, and arrested her for prostitution. Officers transported Jessica to the police department. After an emotional conversation, she explained that she was under the control of a violent and physically abusive panderer. Jessica showed signs of physical trauma. A medical examination revealed a fractured orbital socket, two black eyes, burn marks on both legs, and strangulation marks on her neck. Jessica indicated that her pimp inflicted these injuries when she voiced her desire to stop selling herself. She cooperated with investigators who located and arrested the pimp.

Jessica received the aid of a victim advocate who provided her with safe housing, food, and a change of clothes. The advocate remained close to Jessica through frequent contacts and services and supported her throughout her trafficker's criminal court proceedings. Jessica testified at the trial where the jury found the pimp guilty of several charges, including attempted murder. He is serving a life sentence.

The commitment to Jessica did not end in the courtroom. The victim advocate and members of the vice detail maintain contact with her on a monthly basis. She reconnected with her family outside California and pursued a new career. Anaheim's problem-solving approach enabled Jessica's rescue from the human sex trafficking subculture.

In another undercover vice operation, investigators contacted, arrested, and transported Melissa (fictitious name). Following a long, emotional interview, Melissa decided to save herself. She supplied sufficient evidence for vice investigators to arrest her trafficker. Her victim advocate provided safe housing for the night and transportation home to her family in Florida.

Melissa returned to California to testify in the jury trial against her pimp. She gave compelling testimony, resulting in a conviction. Melissa testified that the victim-centered approach of the vice investigators and her victim advocate helped her escape from the world of prostitution and human trafficking. After her rescue Melissa completed a prostitution rehabilitation program and pursued a new career.

## CONCLUSION

The Anaheim Police Department's priority is recognizing, rescuing, and redirecting the lives of prostituted women. Vice investigators and victim advocates have a positive impact on these situations. This problem-solving approach to reducing street prostitution saves lives.

Maps, graphs, and charts cannot describe the human success stories and incidents of positive life change. The publicity surrounding this problem-solving approach attracted attention, awareness, and contributions from the media, the public, faith-based organizations, local businesses, other law enforcement organizations, and victim advocate agencies. Problem-solving methods impact community problems, but more significantly affect the lives of community members themselves.

Between August 2011, when the project started, and April 30, 2012, the Anaheim vice detail arrested and charged 27 pimps. The courts convicted 16, and 11 await trial. Of the 29 human trafficking victims rescued.

1. 74 percent remain free from subsequent arrest;
2. 3 returned to prostitution;
3. 10 maintain contact with their victim advocates;
4. 2 returned to school;
5. 2 adult victims continue counseling; and
6. 2 continue cooperation with law enforcement and currently are preparing to testify against their traffickers.

The parent of one juvenile victim relocated to a better neighborhood and school district for her daughter. One adult victim stated that she is thankful that she no longer must have sex with strangers. These stories epitomize the Anaheim Police Department's human trafficking project.

### PROGRAM UPDATE
As of October 31, 2012, 38 pimps have been arrested and charged. Twenty were convicted and 18 are awaiting trial. The Anaheim vice detail has rescued 52 human trafficking victims; only 4 are known to have returned to prostitution.

---

### ENDNOTES
[1] Melissa Farley and Howard Barkan, "Prostitution, Violence, and Post Traumatic Stress Disorder," *Women and Health* 27, no. 3 (1998): 37-49.
[2] M. Alexis Kennedy, Carolin Klein, Jessica T.K. Bristowe, Barry S. Cooper, and John C. Yuille, "Routes of Recruitment into Prostitution: Pimps' Techniques and Other Circumstances that Lead to Street

Prostitution," *Journal of Aggression, Maltreatment, and Trauma* 15, no. 2 (2007): 1-19.

3 B. Bullough and V.L. Bullough, "Female Prostitution: Current Research and Changing Interpretations," *Annual Review of Sex Research,* no. 7 (1996): 158-180.

---

## Critical Thinking Exercise

I have personally arrested a number of street prostitutes—women and men—on charges of solicitation for sex or other lewd and lascivious activities. Many of these sex workers were independent; and therefore, did not work at the behest of a pimp or panderer. The APD project described in this article, from my professional view, is right on target. Your assignment is to develop investigative ideas to assist in identifying the true victims of the various forms of human trafficking from independent sex workers. The second component of this exercise is to discuss how non-trafficked prostitutes should be handled in the criminal justice system. In developing your responses, please keep the following thought in mind:

> No one is born to be a prostitute, and those who end up in such a state of misfortune do so for a number of reasons. Some are victims of human or sex trafficking; others are drug addicts funding their fixes and feeding their babies, and others have been sexually, physically, or psychologically abused throughout their lives.

# Human Sex Trafficking

By

Amanda Walker-Rodriguez and Rodney Hill

March 2011: *FBI Law Enforcement Bulletin*

**H**UMAN TRAFFICKING IS THE MOST COMMON FORM OF modern-day slavery. Estimates place the number of its domestic and international victims in the millions, mostly females and children enslaved in the commercial sex industry for little or no money.[1]

The terms Human Trafficking and Sex Slavery usually conjure up images of young girls beaten and abused in faraway places, like Eastern Europe, Asia, or Africa. Actually, human sex trafficking and sex slavery happen locally in cities and towns, both large and small, throughout the United States, right in citizens' backyards.

Appreciating the magnitude of the problem requires first understanding what the issue is and what it is not. Additionally, people must be able to identify the victim in common trafficking situations.

## Human Sex Trafficking

Many people probably remember popular movies and television shows depicting pimps as dressing flashy and driving large fancy cars. More important, the women—adults—consensually and voluntarily engaged in the business of prostitution without complaint. This characterization is extremely inaccurate, nothing more than fiction. In reality, the pimp TRAFFICS young women (and sometimes men) completely against their will by force or threat of force; this is human sex trafficking.

## THE SCOPE

Not only is human sex trafficking slavery but it is big business. It is the fastest-growing business of organized crime and the third-largest criminal enterprise in the world.[2] The majority of sex trafficking is international, with victims taken from such places as South and Southeast Asia, the former Soviet Union, Central and South America, and other less developed areas and moved to more developed ones, including Asia, the Middle East, Western Europe, and North America.[3]

Unfortunately, however, sex trafficking also occurs domestically.[4] The United States not only faces an influx of international victims but also has its own homegrown problem of interstate sex trafficking of minors.[5]

Although comprehensive research to document the number of children engaged in prostitution in the United States is lacking, an estimated 293,000 American youths currently are at risk of becoming victims of commercial sexual exploitation.[6] The majority of these victims are runaway or thrown-away youths who live on the streets and become victims of prostitution.[7] These children generally come from homes where they have been abused or from families who have abandoned them. Often, they become involved in prostitution to support themselves financially or to get the things they feel they need or want (like drugs).

Other young people are recruited into prostitution through forced abduction, pressure from parents, or through deceptive agreements between parents and traffickers. Once these children become involved in prostitution, they often are forced to travel far from their homes and, as a result, are isolated from their friends and family. Few children in this situation can develop new relationships with peers or adults other than the person victimizing them. The lifestyle of such youths revolves around violence, forced drug use, and constant threats.[8]

Among children and teens living on the streets in the United States, involvement in commercial sex activity is a problem of epidemic proportion. Many girls living on the street engage in formal prostitution, and some become entangled in nationwide organized crime networks where they are trafficked nationally. Criminal networks transport these children around the United States by a variety of means—cars, buses, vans, trucks, or planes—and often provide them counterfeit identification to use in the event of arrest. The average age at which girls first become victims of prostitution is 12 to 14. It is not only the girls on the streets who are affected; boys and transgender youth enter into prostitution between the ages of 11 and 13 on average.[9]

### THE OPERATION

Today, the business of human sex trafficking is much more organized and violent. These women and young girls are sold to traffickers, locked up in rooms or brothels for weeks or months, drugged, terrorized, and raped repeatedly.[10] These continual abuses make it easier for the traffickers to control their victims. The captives are so afraid and intimidated that they rarely speak out against their traffickers, even when faced with an opportunity to escape.

Generally, the traffickers are very organized. Many have a hierarchy system similar to that of other criminal organizations. Traffickers who have more than one victim often have a "bottom," who sits atop the hierarchy of prostitutes. The bottom, a victim herself, has been with the trafficker the longest and has earned his trust. Bottoms collect the money from the other girls, discipline them, seduce unwitting youths into trafficking, and handle the day-to-day business for the trafficker.

Traffickers represent every social, ethnic, and racial group. Various organizational types exist in trafficking. Some perpetrators are involved with local street and motorcycle gangs, others are members of larger nationwide gangs and criminal organizations, and some have no affiliation with any one group or organization. Traffickers are not only men—women run many established rings.

Traffickers use force, drugs, emotional tactics, and financial methods to control their victims. They have an especially easy time establishing a strong bond with young girls. These perpetrators may promise marriage and a lifestyle the youths often did not have in their previous familial relationships. They claim they "love" and "need" the victim and that any sex acts are for their future together. In cases where the children have few or no positive male role models in their lives, the traffickers take advantage of this fact and, in many cases, demand that the victims refer to them as "daddy," making it tougher for the youths to break the hold the perpetrator has on them.

Sometimes, the traffickers use violence, such as gang rape and other forms of abuse, to force the youths to work for them and remain under their control. One victim, a runaway from Baltimore County, Maryland, was gang raped by a group of men associated with the trafficker, who subsequently staged a "rescue." He then demanded that she repay him by working for him as one of his prostitutes. In many cases, however, the victims simply are beaten until they submit to the trafficker's demands.

In some situations, the youths have become addicted to drugs. The traffickers simply can use their ability to supply them with drugs as a means of control. Traffickers often take their victims' identity forms, including birth certificates, passports, and drivers' licenses. In these cases, even if youths do leave they would have no ability to support themselves and often will return to the trafficker.

These abusive methods of control impact the victims both physically and mentally. Similar to cases involving Stockholm Syndrome, these victims, who have been abused over an extended period of time, begin to feel an attachment to the perpetrator.[11] This paradoxical psychological phenomenon makes it difficult for law enforcement to breach the bond of control, albeit abusive, the trafficker holds over the victim.

## NATIONAL PROBLEM WITH LOCAL TIES

### THE FEDERAL LEVEL

In 2000, Congress passed the Trafficking Victims Protection Act (TVPA), which created the first comprehensive federal law to address trafficking, with a significant focus on the international dimension of the problem. The law provides a three-pronged approach: PREVENTION through public awareness programs overseas and a State Department-led monitoring and sanctions program; protection through a new T Visa and services for foreign national victims; and PROSECUTION through new federal crimes and severe penalties.[12]

As a result of the passing of the TVPA, the Office to Monitor and Combat Trafficking in Persons was established in October 2001. This enabling legislation led to the creation of a bureau within the State Department to specifically address human trafficking and exploitation on all levels and to take legal action against perpetrators.[13] Additionally, this act was designed to enforce all laws within the 13th Amendment to the U.S. Constitution that apply.[14]

U.S. Immigration and Customs Enforcement (ICE) is one of the lead federal agencies charged with enforcing the TVPA. Human trafficking represents significant risks to homeland security. Would-be terrorists and criminals often can access the same routes and use the same methods as human traffickers. ICE's Human Smuggling and Trafficking Unit works to identify criminals and organizations involved in these illicit activities.

The FBI also enforces the TVPA. In June 2003, the FBI, in conjunction with the Department of Justice Child Exploitation and Obscenity Section and the National Center for Missing and Exploited Children, launched the Innocence Lost National Initiative. The agencies' combined efforts address the growing problem of domestic sex trafficking of children in the United States. To date, these groups have worked successfully to rescue nearly 900 children. Investigations successfully have led to the conviction of more than 500 pimps, madams, and their associates who exploit children through prostitution. These convictions have resulted in lengthy sentences, including multiple 25-year-to-life sentences and the seizure of real property, vehicles, and monetary assets.[15]

Both ICE and the FBI, along with other local, state, and federal law enforcement agencies and national victim-based advocacy groups in joint task forces, have combined resources and expertise on the issue. Today, the FBI participates in approximately 30 law enforcement task forces and about 42 Bureau of Justice Assistance (BJA)-sponsored task forces around the nation.[16]

In July 2004, the Human Smuggling Trafficking Center (HSTC) was created. The HSTC serves as a fusion center for information on human smuggling and trafficking, bringing together analysts, officers, and investigators from such agencies as the CIA, FBI, ICE, Department of State, and Department of Homeland Security.

### THE LOCAL LEVEL

With DOJ funding assistance, many jurisdictions have created human trafficking task forces to combat the problem. BJA's 42 such task forces can be demonstrated by several examples.[17]

- In 2004, the FBI's Washington field office and the D.C. Metropolitan Police Department joined with a variety of nongovernment organizations and service providers to combat the growing problem of human trafficking within Washington, D.C.

- In January 2005, the Massachusetts Human Trafficking Task Force was formed, with the Boston Police Department serving as the lead law enforcement entity. It uses a two-pronged approach, addressing investigations focusing on international victims and those focusing on the commercial sexual exploitation of children.

- The New Jersey Human Trafficking Task Force attacks the problem by training law enforcement in the methods of identifying victims and signs of trafficking, coordinating statewide efforts in the identification and provision of services to victims of human trafficking, and increasing the successful interdiction and prosecution of trafficking of human persons.

- Since 2006, the Louisiana Human Trafficking Task Force, which has law enforcement, training, and victim services components, has focused its law enforcement and victim rescue efforts on the Interstate 10 corridor from the Texas border on the west to the Mississippi border on the east. This corridor, the basic northern border of the hurricane-ravaged areas of Louisiana, long has served as a major avenue of illegal immigration efforts. The I-10 corridor also is the main avenue for individuals participating in human trafficking to supply the labor needs in the hurricane-damaged areas of the state.

In 2007, the Maryland Human Trafficking Task Force was formed. It aims to create a heightened law enforcement and victim service presence in the community. Its law enforcement efforts include establishing roving operations to identify victims and traffickers, deputizing local law enforcement to assist in federal human trafficking investigations, and providing training for law enforcement officers.

ANYTOWN, USA
In December 2008, Corey Davis, the ringleader of a sex-trafficking ring that spanned at least three states, was sentenced in federal court in Bridgeport, Connecticut, on federal civil rights charges for organizing and leading the sex-trafficking operation that exploited as many as 20 females, including minors. Davis received a sentence of 293 months in prison followed by a lifetime term of supervised release. He pleaded guilty to multiple sex-trafficking charges, including recruiting a girl under the age of 18

to engage in prostitution. Davis admitted that he recruited a minor to engage in prostitution; that he was the organizer of a sex-trafficking venture; and that he used force, fraud, and coercion to compel the victim to commit commercial sex acts from which he obtained the proceeds.

According to the indictment, Davis lured victims to his operation with promises of modeling contracts and a glamorous lifestyle. He then forced them into a grueling schedule of dancing and performing at strip clubs in Connecticut, New York, and New Jersey. When the clubs closed, Davis forced the victims to walk the streets until 4 or 5 a.m. propositioning customers. The indictment also alleged that he beat many of the victims to force them to work for him and that he also used physical abuse as punishment for disobeying the stringent rules he imposed to isolate and control them.[18]

As this and other examples show, human trafficking cases happen all over the United States. A few instances would represent just the "tip of the iceberg" in a growing criminal enterprise. Local and state criminal justice officials must understand that these cases are not isolated incidents that occur infrequently. They must remain alert for signs of trafficking in their jurisdictions and aggressively follow through on the smallest clue. Numerous Web sites openly (though they try to mask their actions) advertise for prostitution. Many of these sites involve young girls victimized by sex trafficking. Many of the pictures are altered to give the impression of older girls engaged in this activity freely and voluntarily. However, as prosecutors, the authors both have encountered numerous cases of suspected human trafficking involving underage girls.

The article "The Girls Next Door" describes a conventional midcentury home in Plainfield, New

Jersey, that sat in a nice middle-class neighborhood. Unbeknownst to the neighbors, the house was part of a network of stash houses in the New York area where underage girls and young women from dozens of countries were trafficked and held captive. Acting on a tip, police raided the house in February 2002, expecting to find an underground brothel. Instead, they found four girls between the ages of 14 and 17, all Mexican nationals without documentation.

However, they were not prostitutes; they were sex slaves. These girls did not work for profit or a paycheck. They were captives to the traffickers and keepers who controlled their every move. The police found a squalid, land-based equivalent of a 19th-century slave ship. They encountered rancid, doorless bathrooms; bare, putrid mattresses; and a stash of penicillin, "morning after" pills, and an antiulcer medication that can induce abortion. The girls were pale, exhausted, and malnourished.[19]

Human sex trafficking warning signs include, among other indicators, streetwalkers and strip clubs. However, a jurisdiction's lack of streetwalkers or strip clubs does not mean that it is immune to the problem of trafficking. Because human trafficking involves big money, if money can be made, sex slaves can be sold. Sex trafficking can happen anywhere, however unlikely a place. Investigators should be attuned to reading the signs of trafficking and looking closely for them.

### INVESTIGATION OF HUMAN TRAFFICKING

ICE aggressively targets the global criminal infrastructure, including the people, money, and materials that support human trafficking networks. The agency strives to prevent human trafficking in the United States by prosecuting the traffickers and rescuing and protecting the victims. However, most human trafficking cases start at the local level.

## STRATEGIES

Local and state law enforcement officers may unknowingly encounter sex trafficking when they deal with homeless and runaway juveniles; criminal gang activity; crimes involving immigrant children who have no guardians; domestic violence calls; and investigations at truck stops, motels, massage parlors, spas, and strip clubs. To this end, the authors offer various suggestions and indicators to help patrol officers identify victims of sex trafficking, as well as tips for detectives who investigate these crimes.

## PATROL OFFICERS

Document suspicious calls and complaints on a police information report, even if the details seem trivial.

- Be aware of trafficking when responding to certain call types, such as reports of foot traffic in and out of a house. Consider situations that seem similar to drug complaints.

- Look closely at calls for assaults, domestic situations, verbal disputes, or thefts. These could involve a trafficking victim being abused and disciplined by a trafficker, a customer having a dispute with a victim, or a client who had money taken during a sex act.

- Locations, such as truck stops, strip clubs, massage parlors, and cheap motels, are havens for prostitutes forced into sex trafficking. Many massage parlors and strip clubs that engage in sex trafficking will have cramped living quarters where the victims are forced to stay.

- When encountering prostitutes and other victims of trafficking, do not display judgment or talk down to them. Understand the violent nature in how they are forced into trafficking, which explains their lack of cooperation. Speak with them in a location completely safe and away from other people, including potential victims.

- Check for identification. Traffickers take the victims' identification and, in cases of foreign nationals, their travel information. The lack of either item should raise concern.

## DETECTIVES/INVESTIGATORS

- Monitor Web sites that advertise for dating and hooking up. Most vice units are familiar with the common sites used by sex traffickers as a means of advertisement.

- Conduct surveillance at motels, truck stops, strip clubs, and massage parlors. Look to see if the girls arrive alone or with someone else. Girls being transported to these locations should raise concerns of trafficking.

- Upon an arrest, check cell phone records, motel receipts, computer printouts of advertisements, and tollbooth receipts. Look for phone calls from the jailed prostitute to the pimp. Check surveillance cameras at motels and toll facilities as evidence to indicate the trafficking of the victim.

- Obtain written statements from the customers; get them to work for you.

- Seek assistance from nongovernmental organizations involved in fighting sex trafficking. Many of these entities have workers who will interview these victims on behalf of the police.

- After executing a search warrant, photograph everything. Remember that in court, a picture may be worth a thousand words: nothing else can more effectively describe a cramped living quarter a victim is forced to reside in.

- Look for advertisements in local newspapers, specifically the sports sections, that advertise massage parlors. These businesses should be checked out to ensure they are legitimate and not fronts for trafficking.

- Contact your local U.S. Attorney's Office, FBI field office, or ICE for assistance. Explore what federal resources exist to help address this problem.

OTHER CONSIDERATIONS
Patrol officers and investigators can look for many other human trafficking indicators as well.[20] These certainly warrant closer attention.

## GENERAL INDICATORS

- People who live on or near work premises
- Individuals with restricted or controlled communication and transportation
- Persons frequently moved by traffickers
- A living space with a large number of occupants
- People lacking private space, personal possessions, or financial records
- Someone with limited knowledge about how to get around in a community

## PHYSICAL INDICATORS

- Injuries from beatings or weapons
- Signs of torture (e.g., cigarette burns)

- Brands or scarring, indicating ownership
- Signs of malnourishment

## FINANCIAL/LEGAL INDICATORS

- Someone else has possession of an individual's legal/travel documents
- Existing debt issues
- One attorney claiming to represent multiple illegal aliens detained at different locations
- Third party who insists on interpreting. Did the victim sign a contract?

## BROTHEL INDICATORS

- Large amounts of cash and condoms
- Customer logbook or receipt book ("trick book")
- Sparse rooms
- Men come and go frequently

## CONCLUSION

This form of cruel modern-day slavery occurs more often than many people might think. And, it is not just an international or a national problem—it also is a local one. It is big business, and it involves a lot of perpetrators and victims.

Agencies at all levels must remain alert to this issue and address it vigilantly. Even local officers must understand the problem and know how to recognize it in their jurisdictions. Coordinated and aggressive efforts from all law enforcement organizations can put an end to these perpetrators' operations and free the victims.

## ENDNOTES

[1] HTTP://WWW.ROUTLEDGESOCIOLOGY.COM/BOOKS/H UMAN-SEX-TRAFFICKING-ISBN9780415576789 (accessed

July 19, 2010).

2 HTTP://WWW.UNODC.ORG/UNODC/EN/HUMAN-TRAFFICKING/WHAT-IS-HUMAN- TRAFFICKING.HTMl (accessed July 19, 2010).

3 HTTP://WWW.JUSTICE.GOV/CRIMINAL/CEOS/TRAFFIC KING.HTML (accessed July 19, 2010).

4 Ibid.

5 HTTP://WWW.JUSTICE.GOV/CRIMINAL/CEOS/PROSTIT UTION.HTML (accessed July 19, 2010).

6 Richard J. Estes and Neil Alan Weiner, COMMERCIAL SEXUAL EXPLOITATION OF CHILDREN IN THE U.S., CANADA, AND MEXICO (University of Pennsylvania, Executive Summary, 2001).

7 Ibid.

8 HTTP://FPC.STATE.GOV/DOCUMENTS/ORGANIZATION /9107.PDF (accessed July 19, 2010).

9 Estes and Weiner.

10 HTTP://WWW.WOMENSHEALTH.GOV/ VIOLENCE/TYPES/HUMAN-TRAFFICKING.CFM (accessed July 19, 2010).

11 For additional information, see Nathalie De Fabrique, Stephen J. Romano, Gregory M. Vecchi, and Vincent B. Van Hasselt, "Understanding Stockholm Syndrome," FBI LAW ENFORCEMENT BULLETIN, July 2007, 10-15.

12 Trafficking Victims Protection Act, Pub. L. No. 106-386 (2000), codified at 22 U.S.C. § 7101, et seq.

13 Ibid.

14 U.S. CONST. amend. XIII, § 1: "Neither slavery nor involuntary servitude, except as a punishment for crime whereof the party shall have been duly convicted, shall exist within the United States, or any place subject to their jurisdiction."

15 U.S. Department of Justice, "U.S. Army Soldier Sentenced to Over 17 Years in Prison for Operating a Brothel from Millersville Apartment and to Drug Trafficking," HTTP://WWW.JUSTICE.GOV/USAO/MD/PUB LIC-AFFAIRS/PRESS_RELEASES/PRESS10A.HTM (accessed September 30, 2010).

16 http://www.fbi.gov/about-us/investigate/civilrights/human_trafficking/initiatives (ac cessed September 30, 2010).

17 HTTP://WWW.OJP.USDOJ.GOV/BJA/GRANT/42HTTF.P

DF (accessed September 30, 2010).

[18] HTTP://ACTIONCENTER.POLARISPROJECT.ORG/THE-FRONTLINES/RECENT-FEDERAL-CASES/435-LEADER-OF-EXPANSIVE-MULTI-STATE-SEX-TRAFFICKING-RING-SENTENCED (accessed July 19, 2010).

[19] HTTP://WWW.NYTIMES.COM/2004/01/25/MAGAZINE/25SEXTRAFFIC.HTML (accessed July 19, 2010).

[20] HTTP://HTTF.WORDPRESS.COM/INDICATORS/ (accessed July 19, 2010).

## DISCUSSION QUESTION

As correctly pointed out in this article, Congress enacted the TVPA in 2000. What was the legal authority for Congress to pass such a law, and consequently, for the federal government to be able to investigate and prosecute offenses under this act?

## CRITICAL THINKING EXERCISE

In basic outline form, develop a proactive plan that could be implemented for use by patrol officers and detectives as an aid in indentifying whether any forms of human trafficking or sex slavery exist within a particular jurisdiction.

# SOCIAL NETWORK ANALYSIS
## A SYSTEMATIC APPROACH FOR INVESTIGATING
By Jennifer A. Johnson, Ph.D.,
John David Reitzel, Ph.D., Bryan F. Norwood,
David M. McCoy, D. Brian Cummings,
and Renee R. Tate

March 2013: *FBI Law Enforcement Bulletin*

SOCIAL NETWORK ANALYSIS (SNA) IS OFTEN CONFUSED with social networking sites, such as Facebook, when in fact, SNA is an analytical tool that can be used to map and measure social relations. Through quantitative metrics and robust visual displays, police can use SNA to discover, analyze, and visualize the social networks of criminal suspects.

SNA, a social science methodology, serves as a valuable tool for law enforcement. While technologically sophisticated, SNA proves easy to employ. Using available data, police departments structure the examination of an offender's social network in ways not previously possible.

Manual examination of social networks tends to be difficult, time consuming, and arbitrary, making it more prone to error. SNA provides a systematic approach for investigating large amounts of data on people and relationships. It improves law enforcement effectiveness and efficiency by using complex information regarding individuals socially related to suspects. This often leads to improved clearance rates for many crimes and development of better crime prevention strategies.

SNA derives its value from human organization and social interaction for criminal and noncriminal purposes. Social networks sometimes promote illegal behavior (e.g., juvenile delinquency and gang-related crime) among related offenders across criminal domains. They can provide a source for illicit drug and pornography distribution and international terrorism.[1] The networks may supply an essential first condition for many serious criminal behaviors.

Social networks that enable crime are not mutually exclusive from the networks of law-abiding citizens. They are interspersed within these communities, drawing support from residents and extracting significant costs from host neighborhoods.[2] The influence of social networks in producing criminal behavior indicates that effective crime-fighting strategies are contingent upon law enforcement's ability to identify and respond appropriately to the networks where the behavior is embedded.

### THEORY AND METHOD

SNA is a theory about how humans organize and a method to examine such organization. The approach indicates that actors are positioned in and influenced by a larger social network. Methodologically, it provides a precise, quantitative tool through which agencies can identify, map, and measure relationship patterns.

Three points of data—two actors and the tie or link between them—comprise the basic unit of analysis. Actors "nodes" are people, organizations, computers, or any other entity that processes or exchanges information or resources. Relationships "ties, connections, or edges" between nodes represent types of exchange, such as drug transactions between a seller and buyer, phone calls between two terrorists, or contacts between victims and offenders. SNA focuses on both positive and negative relationships between sets of individuals.

This analysis produces two forms of output, one visual and the other mathematical. The visual consists of a map or rendering of the network, called a social network diagram, which displays the nodes and relationships between them. In larger networks, key nodes are more difficult to identify; therefore, the analysis turns to the quantitative output of SNA.

The centrality of nodes, such as those representing offenders, identifies the prominence of persons to the overall functioning of the network. It indicates their importance to the criminal system, role, level of activity, control over the flow of information, and relationships. Basic centrality metrics provide further details. "Degree" gauges how many connections a particular node possesses, "betweenness" measures how important it is to the flow, and "closeness" indicates how quickly the node accesses information from the network. Nodes are rank ordered according to their centrality, with those at the top playing the most prominent role. These measures cannot tell an analyst what the structure should be, but they can elaborate on the actual makeup of the network. The value and actionable intelligence of each of these metrics is determined by the information the analyst wants.

## CASE STUDY

In January 2008 a collaborative pilot project was launched to explore the viability of incorporating SNA into the precinct-level crime analysis methodologies of the Richmond, Virginia, Police Department (RPD). Participants included representatives of RPD, a university sociologist, and a software designer. The goal was for the research team, comprised of the sociologist and the software designer, to use crime data to assess how constructive SNA would be in solving the most prevalent crimes in the area and to determine the feasibility of training the precinct-level analysts to incorporate it into their workflow.

Researchers needed to determine what initiated violence between two groups of previously friendly young males. Several persons of interest, at one time on good terms, began to argue and assault one another. The source of the violence was not clear, and police were looking for ways to respond. They wanted to know if SNA could help them understand what sparked the violence and which strategies could be developed using a network approach.

The research team received access to RPD's records management system to obtain information on criminal occurrences, arrests, criminal associates, demographics, and victim/offender relationships. The police provided no other background information on the individuals. The research team did not meet or discuss the ongoing investigation with the detectives. Analysis was done off-site, and the only recurring contact was with the police manager to extract the data in relational form.

Using 24 persons of interest labeled by a gang unit detective as "seeds"—starting points, or initially identified persons—the records management system extracted all connections among the seeds from 2007 through October 2008, proceeding four layers out and including any interconnections among the seed and nodes in each step. The connections were categorized by incident type—common incident participation, victim/offender, gang memberships, field contacts, involved others, common locations, and positive or negative connections.

Positive ties included a cooperative relationship between individuals, such as having family connections, robbing a store together, or hanging out. Negative ties indicated hostile relationships, such as those between a victim and offender. Individuals could have multiple and varying connections. Four networks resulted from the sampling, one for each layer out from the seeds. The networks included the seeds, the relationships among them, people directly connected to them, and those related to their associates. This involved 434 individuals and 1,711 ties. Several weak spots existed where a single node connected regions of the network and indicated dense areas of heavy interconnectivity.

Using SNA software, an analyst quickly produced a visual representation, including names, to assess the structure of the group or reference to whom a person of interest was connected. Through visual analysis and examination of the metric of betweenness, analysts located the source of the disagreement. The metric pointed to critical junctures in the network that revealed interpersonal tensions among males revolving around their relationships with females.

Two powerful male gang members reportedly had a positive relationship in October of 2007; however, in April 2008, one victimized a female friend of the other. During the same incident, this male also victimized the female friend of another male. Throughout the episode, a pattern emerged involving situations where a dominant male engaged with a female associate of another strong male. In other words, boys were fighting over girls.

Quantitative metrics provided additional information identifying the powerful players in this network. By rank ordering the individuals according to their centrality measures, the analysis confirmed that the gang unit was watching the right people and using community resources effectively. The metrics also helped unit members further analyze the importance of the seed nodes. Many of the nodes targeted by the unit ranked as powerful in the network based on an SNA metric. The quantitative metrics indicated six other vital players, including one critical to the flow of the network.

## RESULTS

Unanticipated administrative processes delayed the timeline of the pilot project, making these results and recommendations too late to be actionable. The police already had solved the conflict. The knowledge of the detectives, which the research team was not privy to, validated the results. Officers confirmed that the answer the research team had discerned from the data—boys fighting over girls—was the cause of the conflict.

Detectives acknowledged that they would have solved the case more quickly and easily if they had this analysis available to guide their strategies. This feedback validated the worth of the approach and the usefulness of SNA and moved the project into the next phase. Precinct-level crime analysts received training in SNA through a 36-hour, in-house seminar. Through lectures and hands-on training, crime analysts from police and federal agencies used data from their own projects to learn to incorporate SNA to meet their needs. Within 2 weeks of completing the course, the analysts used SNA in several cases, including an aggravated assault/ shooting and several convenience store robberies.

In the shooting incident, the analyst used SNA to provide data on an associate of the suspect who previously was not noticed by the detective working the case. The analyst provided that information to the detective who used it to locate and interview that individual, which put additional pressure on the suspect, who was attempting to elude capture. This, combined with other social and financial pressures, caused the suspect to surrender.

Another case involved a string of convenience store robberies. Using an SNA map of a separate case, an analyst noticed a connection between a person of interest in the robberies in one precinct and a member of the network under investigation. Using the two names as seeds, the analyst extracted another previously unknown network. The analyst and a colleague identified one of the seed names as a person of interest in robberies involving multiple juveniles. Through cooperation and an SNA social diagram, they pieced together robberies not previously thought to be connected and identified a suspect involved in other robberies. The chart provided a source where they quickly, easily, and effectively could share observations with investigative personnel.

### SOCIAL NETWORK DIAGRAMS
Social network diagrams have become a method for RPD to use social relationships among offenders and their associates. Renowned for its technological innovation and policing strategies, RPD has found SNA effective in facilitating better communication between crime analysts and investigators. SNA enabled the department to significantly increase crime clearance rates and reduce violence.

Prior to the SNA training, analysts conceptualized a series of "star" networks with an "ego" at the center and immediate connections radiating out. To understand the network, analysts identified the immediate connections of a person of interest. To identify one of the people connected to the original person of interest, a second ego network was constructed. In the end, the analyst faced a series of networks, leaving out the interconnections between them. Through training, analysts began to interpret the effectiveness of the larger network environment using diagrams as social maps to orient themselves and officers.

In the shooting case, the detective used the network analysis to apply pressure to the suspect by interviewing an associate whose relationship with the offender previously was unknown. Mounting social and financial pressures, ultimately, led the individual to surrender. In the convenience store robberies, an SNA diagram provided vital clues that allowed multiple analysts to share information and identify previously unknown connections between individuals, which led to a possible suspect. If SNA had been available to analysts in other jurisdictions, a connection may have been discovered earlier.

## ANALYSIS

The cases described illustrate the success of SNA in developing law enforcement strategies and interdiction techniques. The pilot project demonstrated how SNA can help answer sophisticated questions regarding motivations for a crime—an area previously underdeveloped in crime analysis processes.[3] The research team was asked to determine why violence occurred among groups who previously were amicable. Using visual analysis and without any subject matter knowledge, investigators used SNA to reveal behavioral motivation rooted in complex interpersonal relationships. The project provided confirmation of the effectiveness of the current resource allocation of the gang unit and indicated new avenues of policing, which have the potential to produce a high return on investment.

These two cases produced actionable results, illustrating how SNA can facilitate a productive working relationship between crime analysts and detectives. The academic research on policing indicated that one of the biggest hurdles in establishing effective communication is finding a common language between the analytics of numbers and the immediate pressures of reality.[4] Each case described illustrates how SNA and social network diagrams function as a common ground. Analysts used the charts visually to depict their analysis, which resonated with detectives because it reflected their reality. The analysts provided something new to the detectives, thus, aiding each investigation.

The visual and quantitative output of SNA helps solve institutional memory issues associated with analysts' longevity and attrition, as well as new hires. By producing a current overview, SNA allows new analysts to grasp the present status of the network. It assists experienced analysts in maintaining an understanding of the network by chronicling growth and development as members and connections appear and disappear.

Law enforcement agencies, such as RPD, benefit from having access to structured, relational, and temporal data. Analysts reliably map changes in the network using an automated extraction process. Through this dynamic procedure, experienced analysts appear less likely to develop data analysis blind spots.

## CONCLUSION

Law enforcement agencies have come a long way from pinpoint mapping. The technological advancements in recent years can provide personnel more confidence to handle complex crime problems confronting departments around the country. Social network analysis demonstrated its utility and effectiveness as a means of solving crimes or determining persons of interest and bridging the gap between crime analysts and police officers in the field. With the support of robust technology, SNA becomes reliable across time, data, analysts, and networks and quickly produces actionable results inside any operational law enforcement environment.

## ENDTEXT
The authors commend and recognize the Richmond, Virginia, Police Department's Crime Analysis Unit for its critical role and ongoing cooperation in the research and writing of this article.

## ENDNOTES
[1] E. Patacchini and Y. Zenou, "The Strength of Weak Ties in Crime," *European Economic Review* 52, no. 2 (2008); D.L. Haynie, "Delinquent Peers Revisited: Does Network Structure Matter?" *American Journal of Sociology* 106, no.4 (2001): 1013-1057; K. Murji, "Markets, Hierarchies, and Networks: Race/Ethnicity and Drug Distribution," *Journal of Drug Issues* 37, no. 4 (2007): 781-804; V. Krebs, "Mapping Networks of Terrorist Cells," *Connections* 24, no. 3 (2004): 43-52; and J.A. Johnson, "To Catch a Curious Clicker: A Social Network Analysis of the Online Commercial Pornography Network" in *Everyday Pornographies*, Karen Boyle, ed. (Routledge Press, 2012).
[2] C. Kadushin, "Who Benefits from Network Analysis: Ethics of Social Network Research" *Social Networks* 27, no. 2 (2005): 139-153.
[3] T.C. O'Shea and K. Nicholls, "Police Crime Analysis: A Survey of U.S. Police Departments with 100 or More Sworn Personnel," *Police Practice and Research* 4, no. 3 (2003): 233-250.
[4] N. Cope, "Intelligence Led Policing or Policing Led Intelligence?" *British Journal of Criminology* 44 (2004): 188-203; and S. Belledin and K. Paletta, "Finding Out What You Don't Know: Tips on Using Crime Analysis," *The Police Chief* 75, no. 9 (2008).

## Discussion Question

From a traditional law enforcement perspective, what do you believe would be good sources of data for SNA?

## Critical Thinking Exercise

For this exercise you need to undertake research to better understand which law enforcement agencies are using SNA, the type of crimes for which it is used, and the results.

# Working Toward the Truth in Officer-Involved Shootings Memory, Stress, and Time

By Geoffrey P. Alpert, Ph.D,
John Rivera, and Leon Lott

May 2012: *FBI Law Enforcement Bulletin*

AN IMPORTANT AREA OF PSYCHOLOGICAL RESEARCH examines "how trauma and other highly emotional experiences can impact perception and memory."[1] Studies indicate that individuals display two distinct ways of processing information into memory: the "rational-thinking mode" during low-emotional states and the "experiential-thinking mode" in a high-stress situation, such as an officer-involved shooting (OIS).[2] This distinction illustrates that the trauma caused by an OIS likely will impact the memories and perceptions of the officers involved.

However, not enough research has been done to determine exactly how these effects distort memories of stressful events. Many studies relate only to routine memory and eyewitness identification, rather than the use of deadly force.[3] Further research must focus on determining how other variables may cause officers' memories of such incidents to vary from reality. Investigators who interview officers following an OIS should remain cautious because their subjects' memories may have been impacted by their experience in numerous and, at times, unpredictable ways.[4] Law enforcement agencies should acknowledge these difficulties when determining protocol for when and how to interview involved officers following an OIS.[5]

## PRIOR RESEARCH

While much study has been conducted on memory and stress, only limited research has focused specifically on how this relates to OIS.[6] These gaps led one researcher to study how memories function differently during traumatic events. To investigate this issue, she surveyed officers over a 6-year period after they had been involved in shooting incidents. Her research found that officers exhibited a variety of reactions and responses to an OIS. For example, more than 60 percent of the officers felt that the incident transpired in slow motion, while 17 percent recalled time speeding up. Over 80 percent of the officers reported auditory lockout, while 16 percent heard intensified sounds.

Similarly, more than 70 percent claimed that they experienced heightened clarity of vision and that they responded to the threat not with "conscious thought," but, rather, on "autopilot." Interestingly, almost 40 percent reported disassociation, while 46 percent reported memory loss. Her findings are both important and consistent with other research indicating that officers experience perceptual and memory distortions during a critical incident, such as an OIS.[7]

Another study also deserves attention. Researchers surveyed 265 police officers from the Midwest who were exposed to three stressful conditions: a live-fire simulation, a video of the training that included the shooting, and a video of the simulation scene without sound or a shooting. Most of the officers were not questioned about their experiences until 12 weeks later, but a sample of the officers participated in a "rehearsal" interview—they answered the questions immediately after the exposure and then again 12 weeks later.

The researchers concluded that, overall, stress was positively related to memories of armed people, unrelated to memories of unarmed people, and negatively related to objects.[8] Their findings echoed other research that suggested eyewitnesses focus on the source of the threat or stress (e.g., the shooter) more intensely than the peripheral information about a scene or incident (e.g., the furniture in the room where the shooting occurred).[9] Interestingly, the study also found that the officers subjected to the immediate rehearsal questioning recalled clearer memories in their second interview 12 weeks later compared with the officers interviewed only once.

This study is important for several reasons. First, it showed that during high-stress events, officers more likely will focus on a threat, rather than peripheral objects or people. If an officer vividly remembers a person with a weapon but has only a blurred vision of an unarmed individual or an object in the room or area, this does not necessarily indicate that the officer's testimony is a conscious deception, planned response, or otherwise illegitimate.

Instead, these distortions may be caused by stress— the research indicated that officers' memories after a traumatic event can play tricks on them or vary from reality. This might result from pressure or anxiety caused by the incident, officers' exhaustion during the event, or other factors that influence memory.[10]

Second, the study supported the argument that it remains unclear as to when officers should be interviewed concerning their observations, actions, and reactions after an OIS. Many ambiguities exist regarding this issue, and, thus, no proven best practices exist for collecting information from officers involved in an OIS.

However, most agencies follow the intuition that exhausted, injured, or otherwise impaired officers should not be questioned immediately after a traumatic event. Otherwise, not only does this pose serious risks to the officers' health and well-being but information gleaned from these interviews may sabotage an investigation. These case studies indicated that through no fault of their own, these officers' memories may suffer from distortions due to the stress caused by such traumatic incidents. As such, investigators must keep these factors in mind when determining the timing and structure of post-OIS interviews.

## AUTHORS' STUDY

To look at this phenomenon more closely, the authors organized a pilot study in December 2010 to examine how officers recall high-stress events. They used the Richland County, South Carolina, Sheriff's Department as the subject of their study. The researchers surveyed officers' reactions to training that involved live-fire simulation and role play by interviewing the officers and analyzing their responses.[11]

The department periodically conducts training activities that involve these live-fire simulations. This instance involved a group of deputies learning to respond to active-shooter situations in schools. The training occurred in an abandoned school that realistically emulated a real world environment. Officers responded to one of two active-shooter scenarios: a school shooting or a terrorist attack. Each simulation involved similar reportable and measurable characteristics.

During the simulation, officers worked in teams to clear a building, assist victims or hostages, and secure suspects. Following the incident, each deputy attended a short debriefing. When the training concluded for the day, half of the officers (Group A) wrote a report detailing the event. Then, the researchers asked Group A to recount the event again 3 days later. The other half of the officers (Group B) were required only to detail their recollections of the event after 3 days passed but were not asked to write a report immediately after the training.

By dividing the subjects into these two groups, the study aimed to determine whether officers' memories were sharper and more accurate in the time immediately following the shooting or sometime later. Also, Group A's rehearsal interview would help illustrate how their memories of a high-stress event changed over time.

Officers' memories were evaluated based on their ability to recall five elements of the event and the level of specificity that they provided. These five items were divided into two categories: threat variables and environmental variables. Each correct assessment of one of these elements earned officers a certain amount of points.

For threat variables, officers received 0 to 3 points for their descriptions of the number, type, and descriptions of weapons. An additional category of threat variables included information on the suspects, including race, gender, and clothing, earning officers another 0 to 4 points. Conversely, for environmental variables, officers earned 0 to 3 points for reporting the location of the incident, including the type of room and surroundings; 0 to 2 points for remembering facts from dispatch, including the nature of the altercation in progress; and another 0 to 2 points for reporting the number and names of other officers on the team.

Each report was assessed based on how accurately the officers could remember the five threat and environmental variables, and the deputies' scores in each category were summed to arrive at an overall score. Then, the total scores of all officers within the two groups were averaged.

## FINDINGS

When officers in Group A detailed the event immediately after the simulation, their total score averaged 7.5 with a high score of 12 and a low score of 4 (out of 14 points possible). Three days later, when Group A's officers provided their recollections for the second time, their average score improved to 7.8 with a high score of 13 and a low score of 4. The total score for Group B's officers, who only provided their recollections 3 days after the simulation, averaged 6.4 with a high score of 10 and a low score of 2.

These results demonstrated that the deputies' memories remained sharper when asked to recount the incident immediately after it occurred, compared with the deputies who were not asked until a few days had passed. Additionally, the memories of individuals asked to share their recollections immediately after the incident improved slightly in their second report.

The researchers analyzed these results further by distinguishing officers' scores for threats versus environmental variables. A separate analysis of these scores (with a maximum score of 7 for each category) showed that the deputies recalled threats more accurately than environmental variables. Group A received an average score of 4.4 for threat variables compared with 3.3 for environmental variables.

Also, the results revealed that officers' recollections of threats weakened slightly over time as their score for threat variables decreased to 4.2. The subjects did not remember environmental variables as accurately in either condition. Group A showed an average score of 3.3 immediately after the event and 3.5 after 3 days passed. Group B averaged 3.3.

Although the differences were not drastic, they demonstrated that, overall, the deputies maintained stronger memories of threats (e.g., the people and weapons that could harm them), rather than the environment (i.e., the conditions under which the event occurred). Additionally, asking officers to recall facts immediately after an event may prove important for collecting accurate threat-related information because the officers' memories of threats weakened slightly after time passed.12 This could suggest that for investigators to obtain the most precise information about an OIS, it might be best for them to ask officers about threat-related information as soon as possible. Conversely, it may not be as urgent to interview witnesses about environmental variables right away.

Because this study involved a simulation, the subjects were not at risk for the same type of exhaustion, injury, or other impairments that can affect officers' memories after a real live-fire incident. But, the major lesson from this pilot study remains that these deputies recalled the threat variables better than environmental factors, and they remembered them best immediately after the incident.

### POLICY IMPLICATIONS
Although a pilot study with significant limitations, this research presents important information for policy makers who determine whether an OIS investigation should involve immediate or delayed interviews of officers. Currently, no law enforcement-wide best practice or proven method exists for the timing of these interviews. However, several influential sources have suggested guidelines.

The Police Assessment Resource Center conducted a study of the Portland, Oregon, Bureau of Police and subsequently recommended that the department's internal affairs investigators interview officers who were involved in or witnessed an OIS no later than a few hours after the event.[13] Conversely, the International Association of Chiefs of Police stated in Police Psychological Services guidelines that investigators should give officers time to recover after the incident before they conduct any detailed interviewing, with this recovery time ranging from a few hours to overnight. Other experts echoed this recommendation; they suggested that officers may make more accurate and thorough statements if they are allowed to wait at least 24 hours before questioning, giving the officers time to rest and recuperate before they make a formal declaration.[14]

Many agencies embraced these suggestions and implemented policies requiring officers to wait before giving an interview or speaking to an investigator about an OIS. In this respect, these departments treat officers differently than they do suspects or civilian witnesses. If agencies think that officers involved in a traumatic event provide better accounts after a waiting period, then why are witnesses and suspects interviewed as soon as possible after the incident?

Prior research consistently determined that individuals' memories react strangely to stressful or traumatic events—officers and civilians alike experience perceptual and memory distortions after these incidents. What remains unknown, however, is what factors influence the distortions and how to minimize them.

To this end, it might be best for agency protocol to allow for case-by-case flexibility when determining the timing and structure of interviews following an OIS. Investigators must remain sensitive to personnel who have just experienced one of the most traumatic events in the life of a police officer but also strive to obtain the most accurate information possible about the incident.

For example, if investigators need precise intelligence about the incident, then it may be important for them to give the officers and civilian witnesses an initial walk-through of the incident without providing details. This walk-through may function as the "rehearsal" interview that helps trigger better memory recall later on as demonstrated in the authors' study. Similarly, an expert highlighted the value of this time delay in the interview process, stating that interviewers can consider "...providing enough brief information during an immediate on-scene 'walk-through' to get the investigation started."[15]

Also, investigators should remain sensitive to the fact that individual officers can react to an OIS differently. Some personnel handle the stress of a shooting better than others, and depending on the outcome of the event, it may be necessary to delay some detailed interviews. For example, if the officers' or witnesses' friends or family suffered injuries, investigators may need to delay asking them to rehash the incident in great detail.

Additionally, if individuals are exhausted, injured, or otherwise impaired, they will not provide meaningful information for any type of fact-finding mission. The decision of when to conduct post-OIS interviews should balance the humanistic concerns for the witnesses with the investigators' need for information.

Even officers employed by the same department and who received the same training may react differently to an OIS; as such, they could display varying levels of detail and accuracy in their recollections of the event. Officers' ages, backgrounds, and life experiences can impact significantly how they will respond to an OIS. Far too often, officers who suffer postshooting trauma feel further pressure from department administrators anxious for information.

This practice could be counterproductive because anything that causes the witness additional stress may hamper memory or recall. Putting pressure on officers by forcing them to recount a traumatic event too soon may result in incomplete and inaccurate information, possibly leading to grave errors in an investigation.

## CONCLUSION

Clearly, more rigorous and precise research must focus on the factors that influence memory distortions and how to minimize them. Researchers have not reached a consensus on how to trigger more accurate memories of stressful events. Additionally, most investigators fail to anticipate the natural distortions, which likely occur due to expected variance rather than deception, that likely will appear in officers' memories. Until a greater understanding of these issues is reached, inconsistencies and inaccuracies in eyewitness testimonies will continue to hamper OIS investigations. Department leaders and personnel alike must acknowledge the many unpredictable factors that influence the memories of the involved officers after an OIS to ensure a successful investigation.

## ENDNOTES

[1] Alexis A. Artwohl, "Perceptual and Memory Distortions in Officer-Involved Shootings," FBI Law Enforcement Bulletin, October 2002, 18-24.

[2] Seymour Epstein, "The Integration of the Cognitive and Psychodynamic Unconscious," American Psychologist 49, no. 8 (1994): 709-724.

[3] Terry Beehr, Lana Ivanitskaya, Katherine Glaser, Dmitry Erofeev, and Kris Canali, "Working in a Violent Environment: The Accuracy of Police Officers' Reports

About Shooting Incidents," *Journal of Occupational and Organizational Psychology* 77 (2004): 217-235.

4 David Hatch and Randy Dickson, *Officer-Involved Shootings and Use of Force: Practical Investigative Techniques* (Boca Raton, FL: CRC Press, 2007).

5 Nelson Cowan and Angela M. AuBuchon, "Short-Term Memory Loss Over Time Without Retroactive Stimulus Interference," *Psychonomic Bulletin Review* 15, no. 1 (2008): 230-235.

6 Matthew Sharpes, *Processing Under Pressure: Stress, Memory and Decision-Making in Law Enforcement* (Flushing, NY: Looseleaf Law Publications, 2009); *AELE Monthly Law Journal*, "Administrative Investigations of Police Shootings and Other Critical Incidents: Officer Statements and Use-of-Force Reports Part Two: The Basics," *http://www.aele.org/law/2008FPAUG/2008-8MLJ201.pdf* (accessed May 3, 2011).

7 Charles A. Morgan III, Gary Hazlett, Anthony Doran, Stephan Garrett, Gary Hoyt, Paul Thomas, Madelon Baranoski, and Steven M. Southwick, "Accuracy of Eyewitness Memory for Persons Encountered During Exposure to Highly Intense Stress," *International Journal of Law and Psychiatry* 27 (2004): 265-279; Alexis A. Artwohl and Loren W. Christensen, *Deadly Force Encounters: What Cops Need to Know to Mentally and Physically Prepare for and Survive a Gunfight* (Boulder, CO: Paladin Press, 1997); R.M. Solomon, "I Know I Must Have Shot, But I Can't Remember," *The Police Marksman,* July/August 1997, 48-51; R.M. Solomon and J.M. Horn, "Post-Shooting Traumatic Reactions: A Pilot Study" in *Psychological Services for Law Enforcement,* ed. J. T. Reese and H.A. Goldstein (Washington, D.C.: U.S. Government Printing Office, 1986), 383-394; D. Grossman and B.K. Siddle, *Critical Incident Amnesia: The Physiological Basis and the Implications of Memory Loss During Extreme Survival Situations* (Millstadt, IL: PPCT Management Systems, 1998); David Klinger, *Into the Kill Zone: A Cop's Eye View of Deadly Force* (San Francisco, CA: Jossey-Bass, 2004); A.L. Honig and J. E. Roland, "Shots Fired: Officer Involved," *The Police Chief,* October 1998, 116-119; and Geoffrey Alpert, Dallas Police Department, *Review of Deadly Force Training and Policies of the Dallas Police Department* (Dallas, TX, 1987).

[8] Terry Beehr, Lana Ivanitskaya, Katherine Glaser, Dmitry Erofeev, and Kris Canali, "Working in a Violent Environment: The Accuracy of Police Officers' Reports About Shooting Incidents," *Journal of Occupational and Organizational Psychology* 77 (2004): 228.

[9] Cowan and AuBuchon, 230-235; David Frank Ross, J. Don Read, and Michael Toglia, ed., *Adult Eyewitness Testimony: Current Trends and Developments* (New York: Cambridge University Press, 1994); and Patricia Yuille and John Tollestrup, "A Model for the Diverse Effects of Emotion on Eye Witness Memory," in *The Handbook of Emotion and Memory: Research and Theory*, ed. S. A. Christianson (New Jersey: Lawrence Erlbaum Associates, 1992), 201-215.

[10] Marian Joëls and Tallie Z. Baram, "The Neuro-Symphony of Stress," *Nature Reviews Neuroscience* 10 (2009): 459-466.

[11] Deputies from numerous divisions in the department attended this training, and, as such, the researchers made no attempt to randomize the subjects or create a sample based on any factors. Additionally, no individual data were collected on the deputies' background or characteristics.

[12] No statistical significance tests were conducted because the purpose of this exercise was to examine the issues, rather than test for significant differences.

[13] Police Assessment Resource Center, *The Portland Police Bureau: Officer-Involved Shootings and In-Custody Deaths* (Los Angeles, CA, 2003).

[14] Grossman and Siddle, *Critical Incident Amnesia: The Physiological Basis and the Implications of Memory Loss During Extreme Survival Situations.*

[15] Artwohl, "Perceptual and Memory Distortions in Officer-Involved Shootings," 22.

## DISCUSSION QUESTIONS

1. The authors ask a great question. For those agencies who believe a 24–48 hour time period should lapse before interviewing an officer in an OIS (for purposes of accuracy), why then do they interview victims and eyewitnesses immediately following the perpetration of the crime?

2. The authors suggest that perhaps one solution to the differences of opinion about when to interview an officer in an OIS, is to handle the matter on a case-by-case basis. What objective criteria might exist to assist in making such a determination on the spot?

## CRITICAL THINKING EXERCISE

As a 25-year-old plainclothes police officer I violated one of the 10 Deadly Errors in law enforcement; I failed to recognize certain "danger signs." Consequently, a serial armed robber caught me off guard and held a large lock blade knife to my throat. But due to my training and experience as a street cop, I had the situation turned around in good order. Two shots took out the bandit who basically took a knife to a gunfight, but didn't know it. As I pulled my concealed snub-nose revolver, the sequence events began to go in slow motion. I definitely had tunnel vision—it was just me or him. I began to experience a mild degree of "detachment" once the threat was over and especially after overhearing an announcement on a police radio that the perpetrator was "DOA." *Based upon these facts, discuss among the team when you think would have been the best time for me to be interviewed by homicide detectives and/or internal affairs investigators, and support your decision.*

## Combating Gangsters Online
### By
### Matthew O'Deane, Ph.D.

April 2011: *FBI Law Enforcement Bulletin*

A S GANG MEMBERS INCREASINGLY USE THE INTERNET, law enforcement personnel need to become more Web savvy. Internet sites, like MySpace, YouTube, Twitter, AIM, and Facebook, continue to grow in such use, and, thus, officers need to understand how to investigate gang-related activity in an online environment.

Many of these Web sites contain information that investigators will find relevant to their cases. Officers can tap into this important source of data by making formal legal requests in a timely manner; this process typically requires a grand jury subpoena, administrative subpoena, court order, search warrant, or user consent pursuant to the Electronic Communications Privacy Act (ECPA) to get the service providers to comply.[1] By exploiting gang members' online activity, investigators use an important weapon in the war against illegal gangs.

### INTERNET COMMUNICATION
Its ease of use, potential audience size, and reduced risk of user detection has made the Internet one of the most prominent methods of gang communication. Gangs of every ethnicity and age group in jurisdictions

across the nation and beyond increasingly take advantage of today's advanced telecommunications capabilities.

Most gang members have a personal Web page (usually through a free Internet service), social networking account, or chat room access. These users can create profile pages, which may include general biographical information; lists of their favorite musicians, books, and movies; photos, at times featuring them and their friends displaying gang-related hand signs or holding weapons; videos of themselves and associates, perhaps even talking openly about their exploits; and links to related Web pages.

They also can send and receive personal messages and communicate privately in chat rooms. The more sophisticated home pages share a number of common elements, such as unique slang; members' e-mail addresses; forums for gangsters' opinions; sections dedicated to honoring deceased members; and links to affiliate gangs' e-mail addresses and Web sites.

Gangsters conduct various types of activity online. Many of them routinely place videos on YouTube featuring them even, at times, singing about their criminal lifestyles. Others advertise prostitutes on the Internet. Members of gangs use Web sites to glorify their group and its members; recruit new gangsters; inform other members of meetings, parties, and other relevant information; commit criminal activity, such as intellectual property crimes, identity theft, and fraud; conduct recruitment activities; provoke rival groups through derogatory postings; and spread their message and culture.

## Variety of Information

Many times, officers will find gang-related Web pages; secure sites that require passwords accessible only to gang members; or links to gangsters' instant messaging, e-mail, audio, or text-messaging services. On other occasions, investigators may locate one via an informant who may provide, if necessary, a name and password needed to access and explore the site. Or, an officer will formally request the needed information.

Gang members' Web pages often help to prosecute them. While pursuing pertinent online information, investigators must understand the law and recognize exactly what they and the service providers can do. Officers also should know how gang members use the Internet and should use against them their desire for recognition and respect in their subculture.

## Basic Subscriber Data

Basic subscriber information may include gangsters' first and last names, user identification number, e-mail address, registered mobile number, Internet protocol (IP) address at the time of sign-up, date and time of account creation, and most recent logins (generally the last 2 to 3 days prior to processing the request). In general, successful data retrieval depends on the investigator finding a gangster's user ID, group ID, or the associated user name or group name; officers can locate this information by checking the e-mail addresses connected with gang members' accounts.

The author has had success by accessing and exploring informants' accounts (upon gaining their consent) to find information on targets—often fellow gang members—of investigations and then taking the necessary steps to gain additional data (e.g., a user's name, date of birth, address, gender, and private message information). When dealing with service providers, investigators will benefit by having valuable information up front. Requests without specifics typically require more time and effort to identify a particular user account. Generally, officers will need a court order under Title 18, U.S. Code, Section 2703 (d); a search warrant; or user consent.

## IP LOG-IN RECORDS

Investigators can access logs showing the IP address assigned to users and the dates and times that they accessed their profiles. The process required to obtain historical records typically includes a grand jury subpoena or administrative subpoena under Title 18, U.S. Code, Section 2703 (c)(2); a court order; a search warrant; or user consent. Prospectively capturing log-in IPs typically requires a pen register/trap-and-trace order under Title 18, U.S. Code, Section 3121.

## PRIVATE MESSAGES

Private messages in a gangster's inbox remain available until the individual removes them. Service providers do not maintain copies of messages marked for deletion by a user and cannot recover them once deleted. And, without an already operational Title III wiretap, investigators have no access to them. Gang members' private messages not manually deleted stay in the sent box for 14 days. Additionally, bulletins sent from and held for users on service provider servers are available.

To obtain messages less than 180 days old, investigators need a search warrant under Title 18, U.S. Code, Section 2703 (a); or user consent. For older messages, officers need a subpoena or court order where the government provides prior notice to the subscriber (or delays notice under Title 18, U.S. Code, Section 2705), a search warrant, or user consent. For example, an investigator may present a warrant asking the provider for records pertaining to a particular user ID, including the person's name, postal code, country, and e-mail address; date of account creation; IP address at account sign-up; logs showing IP address and date stamps for account accesses; and the contents of the user's inbox and sent mail folder.

## PHOTOPRINT

The photoprint is a compilation of all photos uploaded and not deleted by the user, along with those uploaded by another individual and featuring a tag of the user of interest. A request should specify photo prints related to a particular user ID. Officers should remember that these pictures typically are delivered in PDF format and contain profile information, such as links to other photos, videos, and blogs. The process required to get this information involves a grand jury or administrative subpoena; court order in which the government provides prior notice to the subscriber under Title 18, U.S. Code, Section 2703 (b)(2) (or delays notice under Title 18, U.S. Code, Section 2705); search warrant; or user consent.

## VIDEOS

Gang members often post videos of themselves, sometimes conducting incriminating activity, on Web sites, such as YouTube. These videos provide an excellent way to prove that individuals in an investigation are gang members. As the videos are public domain, they need simply to be downloaded. Later, they can serve as valuable evidence for a jury.

## FORENSIC EVIDENCE

In many cases, a tremendous amount of information, such as instant messenger chat and client logs, may exist on the gangster's personal computer—of course, not in the possession of the service provider. Cookie data can remain on a gangster's computer for extended periods of time if the individual did not clear it after using the machine to access an ISP account. Investigators easily can find that information. The same is true with cached pages—electronic copies of viewed pages—stored on the local machine until the user or computer removes them. This can include viewed images. To obtain such information, investigators should include personal computers in all gang-related search warrants when appropriate and should search and seize the machines in accordance with these warrants to gather as much evidence against a gangster as possible. These search warrants are defined under Title 18, U.S. Code, Section 2703.

## Location Tools

Investigators also can take advantage of applications that can allow someone to locate a cellular telephone from a computer or another cell phone. While designed to locate a lost cellular device, these applications can find a potential victim just as well. For a nominal cost, officers can have a program that not only will follow people in real time but provide turn-by-turn directions on how to get to them. Gangsters often want their friends to know where they are, but, if their friends know, so can their enemies. Many of these individuals add a location to their tweets letting all of their friends know where they are. This, of course, can be used by rival gang members to find or set them up by intercepting tweets or by having associates pass these messages along to them.

## Procurement Procedures

For information requests, service providers need the identity of requesting officers; their agency; employer-issued e-mail address; telephone contact, including area code and extension; and department mailing address (a post office box often will prove insufficient). They also must have a response due date, which typically should allow them at least two to four weeks for processing. Service providers also should receive from investigators specific details pertaining to the account, such as dates of interest—data pertaining to large periods of time may be unavailable or labor intensive to retrieve.

Most of the communication between the requesting officer and the service provider will be via e-mail, including the returned data, which also may be mailed on storage media.

Many times, such requests involve costs that may need management approval. Service providers typically reserve the right to charge reasonable fees, where permissible, to cover the cost of replying to user data requests, such as search warrants or subpoenas. Title 18, U.S. Code, Section 2706, defines and governs these compensation matters. This does not require government agencies seeking certain categories of information to pay for subpoena compliance unless the request is overly burdensome.

## SEARCH WARRANTS

As with all warrants, investigators need to explain why they need the information. For example, officers may want to tell the judge that based on their training and experience, they know that gang members and their crimes are inherently conspiratorial in nature and involve continual and regular contact between the gangsters. As such, the investigators would believe that by securing the requested information for the appropriate time period that they will collect sufficient evidence to identify the criminals.

And, just like every other search warrant, officers need to identify the account information of interest and the items they intend to seize. Further, investigators should specify the address, but include language covering *all* storage locations owned, maintained, controlled, or operated by the provider. This is in case the data is stored at a location other than the headquarters address.

## EMERGENCY DISCLOSURES

Web providers voluntarily can disclose information, including user identity, log-in information, private messages, and other data, to federal, state, or local authorities when they believe in good faith that an emergency involving danger of death or serious physical injury to any person requires such disclosure without delay. Emergency disclosures must meet the threshold requirements of the ECPA as demonstrated in writing by the requestor. Law enforcement officers must be careful not to include a promise of future process or sign forms that promise such.

In these situations, service providers will supply information pursuant to Title 18, U.S. Code, Sections 2702 (b)(6)(C) and 2702 (c)(4). Emergency disclosures are not compelled, but voluntary on the part of the provider, who may refuse without legal consequence. Often, they seek information, the amount of their choice, to enable them to determine whether an emergency exists. Typically, an emergency disclosure statement by law enforcement, including a description of the nature of the emergency (e.g., potential bodily harm or kidnapping), is required; and, even though the guidelines may vary slightly between service providers, most require essentially the same facts.

Pursuant to Title 18, U.S. Code, Sections 2702 (b)(7) and 2702 (c), officers need to give as much information as possible to persuade the provider to supply the information needed. Investigators should seek only information they believe will assist them in protecting those potentially affected by the emergency. Officers must attest that the request is true and accurate to the best of their knowledge and sign the request.

User Consent
Similar to when they knock on doors and ask for consent to search, officers can do essentially the same with Internet service providers. Information can be obtained pursuant to the voluntary consent of the user per Title 18, U.S. Code, Sections 2702 (b)(3) and 2702 (c)(2). Authentication of the true identity of the user must be provided and articulated in the consent request (e.g., a notarized consent letter).

## OTHER REQUESTS

Disabling Accounts
Most providers will not disable an account if it will jeopardize an ongoing investigation. Officers not wanting targets to know that their account is being investigated should clearly specify not to disable an account until a particular date. Conversely, investigators who want an account disabled immediately—to stop threats, for example—and who do not care if the target knows can indicate that it is not a problem to disable the account.

Preserving Records
In accordance with Title 18, U.S. Code, Section 2703 (f), providers must comply with requests by law enforcement to preserve information for 90 days with an extension for another 90 days upon a renewed request per Title 18, U.S. Code, Section 2703 (f)(2). Pending the issuance of a subpoena or search warrant, providers will preserve information in accordance with the law but will not produce data until receipt of a valid legal request. When service providers receive a preservation request, they merely save a copy of the information they possess, which will be retained and later provided to law enforcement upon presentation of legal process. However, investigators should note that gangsters can continue modifying the information on

their page as before and that these actions will not affect the stored copy retained by the service provider.

Officers should not routinely seek preservation of all data, only what they intend to obtain through the legal process. Otherwise, providers will be preserving, in some cases, a vast amount of data, perhaps not valuable to law enforcement personnel.

Officers should tell service providers that failure to comply with the request could subject them to liability under Title 18, U.S. Code, Section 2707 and ask that they do not disclose the existence of the request to the subscriber or any other person unless necessary. Investigators also must ensure that they provide a means for providers to contact them; they further should thank these individuals for cooperating. Once information in an active account has been preserved, the account will remain active, and the user will not be prevented from logging into it. Any request to restrict the user's access to the profile should be based on investigators' assessment of whether this would impede the investigation.

CASE EXAMPLES

To gain a greater understanding of how gang members' online activities can help in investigations, officers can benefit from real-world examples. To this end, the author offers three cases.

## Case #1

A gang member testified in court against his associates who committed two murders. Just prior to taking the stand, the witness received threats via instant messaging, which he relied on to stay updated about goings-on in the gang. Particularly disturbing were a common greeting for his fellow gang members followed by a threat to his family and a listing of his home address. Clearly, this situation demanded immediate attention.

With the witness' consent, the author examined the phone and obtained the necessary information to get a warrant to identify the source of the threats. The service provider was contacted, and a warrant was drafted that resulted about five hours later in the identification of the account holder sending the threats. The following day, the fugitive task force arrested this individual.

As it turned out, a gangster in court had been relaying information to a fellow gang member in another state. This individual then forwarded the texts to the witness in an attempt to get him to recant or fail to testify. Fortunately, it did not work. The witness took the stand and testified, and a bold statement was made to the gang: Those who make threats against a witness in a gang case—in person or online—will be held accountable for their actions.

## Case #2

In another case, four gang members arrested for involvement in a shooting were awaiting trial in county jail. All initially claimed they were not active members. However, a visitor took cell phone pictures subsequently posted on MySpace of two of them throwing up gang signs while waiting in a holding tank for the trial to begin. Once confronted with the photos, they stopped their denials of gang affiliation. Further, investigators knew when and where the photos were taken.

## Case #3

On a Web page, a gang member had pictures of himself holding several guns and communicating that he was on a "murder mission." He provided his gang name, moniker, and specific photos showing his tattoos; his identity and home address later were determined. After a short surveillance, officers arrested him and conducted a search of his car and home, finding several guns and a lot of gang evidence. The arrest never would have been made if not for the creative and proactive approach taken by investigators to use the gang's desire for recognition against them.

## CONCLUSION

Investigators have access to much information online that can help them in their cases against gang members. A search of the cyber world should be part of every major gang investigation; it should not be an untapped resource in any jurisdiction. Officers should take advantage of the information superhighway to make the community safer and successfully prosecute gangsters by using against them their desire to be well-known, respected, and feared. It takes effort and time but has proven in many cases to be well worth it.

## ENDNOTES

[1] Title 18, U.S. Code, Section 2701, *et seq*. For additional guidance on the issues discussed in this article, access the Web site of the U.S. Department of Justice, Computer Crime and Intellectual Property Section (CCIPS) at *http://www.cybercrime.gov/*.

## Critical Thinking Exercise

In November 2013, two men were convicted of making terroristic threats, intimidating witnesses, and participating in criminal conspiracy based upon a song they posted on YouTube. The lyrics the men sang included threats against two Pittsburgh police officers who were involved in the arrest of convicted cop-killer Richard Poplawski. The men even went as far as to praise Poplawski. The defense had relied unsuccessfully on the First Amendment's protection of freedom of speech. There have been several U.S. Supreme Court cases that articulate the notion that different forms of speech have different degrees of protection under the First Amendment. For example, books and movies normally have higher levels of protection than live productions and shows. Your assignment in this case is to research the matter and attempt to ascertain where direct or implied threats on a YouTube posting fit within the Supreme Court's dual hierarchies:  1) the nature of what is said; and 2) the mechanism for the delivery of the statement (e.g., book, newspaper, television, movie, live performance, etc.)

# CHILD ABDUCTIONS:
# KNOWN RELATIONSHIPS ARE THE GREATER DANGER

By Ashli-Jade Douglas

August 2011: *FBI Law Enforcement Bulletin*

ACCORDING TO THE NATIONAL CENTER FOR MISSING and Exploited Children (NCMEC), every year, more than 200,000 children are abducted by family members. An additional 58,000 are taken by nonrelatives with primarily sexual motives. However, only 115 reported abductions represent cases in which strangers abduct and kill children, hold them for ransom, or take them with the intention to keep.[1]

Media news outlets have portrayed that abductors primarily consist of strangers or registered sex offenders (RSO), which has proven invalid in the past 2 fiscal years (FY). When a child is reported missing, members of the media advise parents to check sex offender registries to prevent their child from possible abduction or sexual victimization. However, FBI reporting indicates that RSOs are a minimal part of the problem. In FY 2009, an RSO was the abductor in 2 percent of child abduction cases; in FY 2010, this figure dropped to 1 percent.[2]

Although parents teach their children to stay away from strangers, most neglect to teach them not to allow anyone, even someone they know, to take them without parental consent. Additionally, children frequently are instructed to obey elders without question, adding to their vulnerability to offenders known to the child victim.

Over the past 4 years, the FBI has seen a decrease in abductions committed by a stranger or RSO. However, it is important to note that abductors with sexual intentions are, in fact, sexual offenders who have not yet been identified and, therefore, are unknown to local law enforcement agencies.

A majority (68 percent) of the child abduction cases the FBI's Child Abduction Rapid Deployment (CARD) team has assisted in has resulted in the identification of an offender who had a relationship with the child victim.[3] Moreover, an RSO was involved in only 10 percent of the investigations, 5 percent of who knew the victim.

In FY 2009, 63 percent of child abduction cases involved an offender known to the victim; only 1 percent were RSOs.[4] In FY 2010, 70 percent of child abduction cases resulted in the identification of an offender who had a known relationship with the victim; less than 1 percent of the abductors were RSOs.[5]

RSOs contribute to a miniscule part of the child abduction problem. In contrast to media reporting, the number of cases involving a registered sex offender is decreasing. In addition to the FBI reporting, NCMEC has revealed that there were no RSOs involved in AMBER Alert cases in 2009.[6]

Although abductors can vary in age, race, or physicality, the FBI assesses with high confidence that the majority of child abductors involved in FBI child abduction cases, CARD team deployments, and AMBER Alerts have a relationship with the child victim. Moreover, despite media reporting, the FBI confidently assesses that the majority of child abductions are committed by persons with a relationship to the child they abduct.

## ENDNOTES

[1] National Center for Missing and Exploited Children, press release, May 18, 2009; http://www.missingkids.com/missingkids/servlet/NewsEventServlet?LanguageCountry= en_US&PageId=4046 (accessed April 26, 2011).

[2] For the purpose of this article, the author defines abduction as "the initial report of a child taken without the knowledge of a parent or guardian."

[3] The FBI's Child Abduction Rapid Deployment (CARD) team was established in 2009 to provide FBI field offices with a resource team of additional investigators with specialized experience in child abduction matters. These regional teams provide rapid, on-site response to provide investigative, technical, and resource assistance during the most critical time period following a child abduction. In 2009, the team had the most deployments since its inception.

[4] Based on FBI investigations.

[5] Ibid.

[6] National Center for Missing and Exploited Children, 2009 AMBER Alert Report; http://www.missingkids.com/en_US/documents/2009AMBERAlertReport.pdf (accessed April 26, 2011).

*Ms. Douglas is an intelligence analyst with the FBI's Criminal Investigative Division*

## Critical Thinking Exercise

Based upon the information provided in this article, how can these data be useful in decreasing even more the incidences of child abduction? Your assignment is to use these data in order to develop (in outline form), a plan by which you seek to: 1) decrease the number of child abductions; and 2) more quickly identify the offender and rescue the child.

# CYBERBULLYING AND SEXTING:
# LAW ENFORCEMENT PERCEPTIONS

By

## Justin W. Patchin, Ph.D., Joseph A. Schafer, Ph.D., and Sameer Hinduja, Ph.D.

June 2013: *FBI Law Enforcement Bulletin*

LAW ENFORCEMENT OFFICERS OFTEN STRUGGLE TO determine their proper role in addressing bullying behavior. Emerging social networking and other communication tools and their accompanying roles in the shift in youth behavior complicate the situation. Historically, bullying occurred within or in close proximity to a school or neighborhood; however, technology allows present-day bullies to extend their reach.

## PROBLEM

Defined as "willful and repeated harm inflicted through the use of computers, cell phones, and other electronic devices," cyberbullying has become a growing concern.[1] It includes sending threatening texts, posting or distributing libelous or harassing messages, and uploading or distributing hateful or humiliating images or videos to harm someone else.[2] Estimates of the number of youth who experience cyberbullying range from 5 to 72 percent, depending on the age of the group and the definition of cyberbullying.[3]

Sexting is another issue involving teens and technology that poses a public concern. Sexting involves "sending or receiving sexually explicit or sexually suggestive nude or seminude images or video, generally via cell phone."[4] Often individuals initially send these images to romantic partners or interests, but the pictures can find their way to others.[5] Estimates of the number of youth who have participated in sexting range from 4 to 31 percent.[6] In 2010 surveys from 4,400 middle and high school students indicated that 8 percent had sent naked or seminude images of themselves to others, and 13 percent reported receiving such pictures from classmates.[7]

Cyberbullying and sexting are significant problems facing teens and schools because of the psychological, emotional, behavioral, and physical repercussions that can stem from victimization.[8] School administrators recognize the severity of these issues, and promising practices provide these educators what they need to know about cyberbullying and sexting, their prevention, and the proper responses when incidents arise. Questions of law enforcement's role linger and deserve an answer.

## SURVEY

Law enforcement officers, especially those assigned to school settings, likely will encounter cyberbullying, sexting, and other forms of online impropriety. The authors collected two separate samples for their investigation of these problems. The first, taken in May 2010, involved 336 school resource officers (SROs) who completed an online survey about cyberbullying and sexting. The second sample included law enforcement leaders attending the FBI National Academy (FBINA), a 10-week residential career development experience at the FBI Academy in Quantico, Virginia. The authors collected data from surveys administered to 643 officers from three FBINA classes in 2010 and 2011.

The SRO and FBINA samples were predominantly male (77 percent and 92 percent respectively) and Caucasian (82 percent and 83 percent) with 73 percent being between the ages of 36 and 50 years old. The FBINA participants averaged 20 years experience in law enforcement, compared with 15 years for the SROs. Twenty-three percent of FBINA participants and 95 percent of SROs had school assignment experience. Both groups responded to comparable surveys on experiences with cyberbullying and sexting cases, as well as perceptions of their primary professional role in preventing and responding to such incidents.

## SCHOOL RESOURCE OFFICERS

Ninety-four percent of SROs agreed that cyberbullying was a serious problem warranting a law enforcement response. Seventy-eight percent stated that they conducted cyberbullying investigations (an average of 16 separate incidents) during the previous school year. Of the 336 respondents, 93 percent indicated that sexting was an important concern for law enforcement officers. Sixty-seven percent reported investigating an average of five sexting incidents in the previous year.

Approximately 50 percent of the SROs commented that the school in which they worked had a policy on cyberbullying; however, only 25 percent said there was a sexting policy. Eighteen percent of the respondents were unsure whether there were policies in place.

Officers reported that most cyberbullying occurred through social networking or text messaging. One officer described an incident that involved female students spreading defamatory information about one classmate's sexual activities, choice of boyfriends, and other associations. Officers, school administrators, and parents worked together to alleviate the problem by advising the involved students that their behavior possibly could be criminal and that subsequent harassment would involve the court system.

Generally, sexting incidents involve romantic partners. One SRO stated that boyfriends and girlfriends send pictures to each other, sometimes with the boy sharing the girl's photos with his friends. Images sent and received as part of a consensual relationship received informal handling with officers talking to students and parents about the seriousness of the situation. When coercion or unauthorized distribution occurred, formal prosecution was likely. An officer conveyed a situation where a girl made an obscene video for her boyfriend, who distributed it to multiple other people, resulting in a child pornography investigation.

### FBI NATIONAL ACADEMY PARTICIPANTS

Eighty-two percent of the FBINA respondents recognized that cyberbullying was a significant issue necessitating police involvement. Ten percent of the officers indicated that they had experience investigating cyberbullying cases, averaging two cases during the previous school year. While 78 percent of the FBINA respondents determined that sexting was a considerable concern for law enforcement, only 7 percent (averaging three cases each in the previous year) reported that they investigated sexting incidents.

### RESEARCH FINDINGS

Using hypothetical cyberbullying scenarios (table 1), all respondents rated the extent to which law enforcement should play a significant role. They perceived the greatest law enforcement role in situations involving a threat of physical harm. For example, they used a scale with 0 being no role and 10 being a significant role to rate the appropriate responsibility of officers in the following situation: A male student received an e-mail from an unknown person threatening to kill him at school the next day. The average rating was 9.1 for the SROs and 8.6 for the FBINA respondents.

Participants indicated that a formal law enforcement response was not essential in situations involving potential violations of student codes of conduct. They rated the following scenario: A teacher confiscates a cell phone from a student in class and wants to determine if it contains any information that is in violation of school policy. SROs rated the law enforcement role on average as 2.4, and FBINA respondents reported 1.4. Law enforcement officers understand their role more clearly when the behavior is an obvious violation of state or local law and less if there is no immediate safety concern.

**Law Enforcement Perceptions Regarding Responsibility in Dealing with Cyberbullying**

| With 0 being no law enforcement role or responsibility and 10 being a very important or significant role or responsibility, to what degree should law enforcement be involved? | School Resource Officers N=336 Mean | FBI National Academy N=643 Mean |
|---|---|---|

| | | |
|---|---|---|
| A male student receives an e-mail from an unknown person threatening to kill him at school tomorrow. | 9.1 | 8.6 |
| A female student, Jenny, covertly takes a picture of another female student, Margaret, in her underwear in the girl's locker room and posts it on a website without permission that allows the rest of the student body to rate or judge Margaret's physical appearance. | 8.9 | 7.8 |
| A parent calls to report that her son has a naked image of a female student from his school on his cell phone. | 8.3 | 6.3 |
| A parent calls the police department to report that her son is being cyberbullied by another youth in their neighborhood. | 7.8 | 6.5 |

| | | |
|---|---|---|
| A student creates a Facebook Fan Page called "Give Mary a Wedgie Day." Mary is a student at a school in your jurisdiction. | 5.8 | 3.8 |
| A male student reveals another classmate's sexual orientation (without permission) via Twitter to the rest of the student body. | 5.7 | 4.0 |
| A female student receives a text message from another classmate calling her a slut. | 4.2 | 3.4 |
| A student creates a webpage making fun of the school principal. | 4.1 | 2.6 |
| A teacher confiscates a cell phone from a student in class and wants to determine if it contains any information that violates school policy. | 2.4 | 1.4 |

N=Number of respondents

Experience with cyberbullying and sexting cases, gender of the officer, and whether the officer had young children living at home all were predictors of perceptions about the role of law enforcement. Officers who recently investigated a cyberbullying or sexting case were more likely to view these issues as a significant law enforcement concern. This finding explains why SROs reported a greater law enforcement role than the FBINA respondents in all of the scenarios. SROs had direct experience with cyberbullying and sexting. Female officers and police with children aged 18 or younger living at home agreed that law enforcement played a significant role in dealing with these problems.

The research indicated that more young people will encounter a cyberbully than be groomed, abducted, and assaulted by a stranger on the Internet.[9] However, over 80 percent of study participants indicated that they needed additional training on preventing and responding to cyberbullying. Twenty-five percent of the SROs and over 40 percent of the FBINA officers surveyed did not know if their state had a law specific to cyberbullying. As of this writing, 49 states had laws regarding bullying, and 45 of those mentioned electronic forms of harassment.[10]

### BEST PRACTICES

Law enforcement officers, especially SROs, need an awareness and understanding of their state statutes to grasp the legal implications of cyberbullying. The growth of cell phones and Internet usage among teens has altered youth social and conduct norms. Cyberbullying is one of the most significant new issues law enforcement has to address. Anecdotal and research-based accounts from police across the nation depicted a lack of clear guidance, training, and support. This is unfortunate because bullying is an age-old problem with recent forms often relying on technological devices and mediums. Research has indicated a strong link between online and offline bullying.[11]

Even if no criminal statute on cyberbullying exists, law enforcement should not ignore these behaviors or dismiss the issue. Officers must help other professionals, such as school administrators, understand legal obligations and authority regarding cyberbullying. School officials can discipline students for their behavior when there is a policy prohibiting such conduct—even when the student is away from campus—if the official can demonstrate that the behavior substantially disrupted the learning environment at school.[12]

When educating the community about cyberbullying, law enforcement officers should stress that different levels of responsibility exist; the matter is serious; an investigation will occur; and parents, schools, and the criminal justice system could punish the offender if warranted.

Online harassment not covered by specific cyberbullying laws may fall under traditional statutes. Officers have charged students for disorderly conduct in incidents that interrupt the main educational purpose of schools (e.g., making embarrassing videos at school and distributing them online) or infringe upon the rights of others. It is important for authorities to take cyberbullying situations more seriously that appear motivated by race, class, gender, or sexual orientation. While directed solely at one person, these events reflect malice and bias toward an entire group of people. Police should consult their district attorney liaisons to determine what existing criminal statutes apply.

Criminal law often pertains when stalking, coercion, sexually explicit images, or the sexual exploitation of youth are involved. High-profile cases of criminal prosecution against teens who engage in sexting illustrate the complexity of addressing this behavior. Legal and political authorities often factor in the age of participants and the relational context in which the sexting incident occurred.[13] Many states have introduced or enacted legislation that addresses sexting, with penalties ranging from educational programming for first-time offenders to fines, felony charges, or short-term incarceration.[14] Sexting occurs along a continuum, ranging from typical teenage behavior to significant and intentional victimization of others.[15]

Due to the sensitive nature of the images and the potential for these photos to remain publicly available, law enforcement involvement at all levels is important.

CONCLUSION

Law enforcement officers, especially those assigned to schools, are called upon to act after incidents and will need to address cyberbullying at some point during their tenure. Even if the cyberbullying behavior is not at a criminal level, officers should handle the situation in a way that is appropriate for the circumstances. A discussion of the legal issues may be enough to deter some first-time bullies from future misbehavior. Officers should talk to parents about their child's conduct and the seriousness of online harassment. Law enforcement's response will vary based on how the case was discovered, what harm has occurred, how evidence was collected, who was involved, and what level of training officers have received.

Cyberbullying and sexting still are relatively new social problems, and officers involved in this study agreed that they need more training to help them understand and respond to these behaviors. Some participants perceived that when these issues occurred away from school, the school could not take any action. One school resource officer stated, "The incident began on Facebook and was done outside of school hours, so the school was unable to do anything about the cyberbullying." Another noted, "Most of the time the school district does not get involved because cyberbullying does not happen on school time." A third officer pointed out that "Most of these occurred outside of school, so there was no school punishment."

It is important that law enforcement officers understand that schools can discipline students for their off-campus behavior when it infringes on the rights of other students or results in or has a foreseeable likelihood of causing substantial and material disruption of the learning environment of the school.[16] Even when the behavior does not violate the law, schools can and should apply appropriate discipline. Law enforcement officers play an important role in ensuring that proper responses are provided to minimize the future risk and harm that cyberbullying and sexting may create.

*The authors would like to thank John Jarvis of the FBI and the Police Futures International/FBI Futures Working Group for helping to make this project possible. The data for this work were collected as part of the Futurist In-Residence Program.*

**ENDNOTES**
[1] Sameer Hinduja and J.W. Patchin, *Bullying Beyond the Schoolyard: Preventing and Responding to Cyberbullying* (Thousand Oaks, CA: Sage Publications, Corwin Press, 2009), p. 5.
[2] Sameer Hinduja and J.W. Patchin, *Bullying Beyond the Schoolyard*, p. 5.
[3] J.W. Patchin and Sameer Hinduja, *Preventing and Responding to Cyberbullying: Expert Perspectives* (Thousand Oaks, CA: Routledge, 2012).
[4] Sameer Hinduja and J.W. Patchin, *School Climate 2.0: Reducing Teen Technology Misuse by Reshaping the Environment* (Thousand Oaks, CA: Sage Publications, Corwin Press, 2012).

[5] L.E. Soronen, N. Vitale, and K.A. Haase, "Sexting at School: Lessons Learned the Hard Way, Inquiry and Analysis," *http://www.nsba.org/* (accessed January 30, 2013); J. Leshnoff, "Sexting, Not Just for Kids," *http://www.aarp.org/relationships/love-sex/info-11-2009/sexting_not_just_for_kids.html* (accessed January 30, 2013); and J. Wolak and D. Finkelhor, "Sexting: A Typology," *http://www.unh.edu/ccrc/pdf/CV231_Sexting%20Typology%20Bulletin_4-6-11_revised.pdf* (accessed January 30, 2013).

[6] S. Hinduja and J.W. Patchin, *Reducing Teen Technology*; V. Stuart-Cassel, A. Bell, and J.F. Springer, "Analysis of State Bullying Laws and Policies," *http://www2.ed.gov/rschstat/eval/bullying/state-bullying-laws/state-bullying-laws.pdf* (accessed January 30, 2013).

[7] S. Hinduja and J.W. Patchin, *Reducing Teen Technology*.

[8] M.L. Ybarra, M. Diener-West, and P.J. Leaf, "Examining the Overlap in Internet Harassment and School Bullying: Implications for School Intervention," *Journal of Adolescent Health* 41 (2007): S42-S50; and S. Hinduja and J.W. Patchin, "Bullying, Cyberbullying, and Suicide," *Archives of Suicide Research* 14, no. 3 (2010): 206-221.

[9] J.G. Palfrey, D. Boyd, and D. Sacco, "Enhancing Child Safety and Online Technologies: Final Report of the Internet Safety Technical Task Force," (Durham, NC: Carolina Academic Press, 2009).

[10] S. Hinduja and J.W. Patchin, "Bullying and Cyberbullying Laws," *http://www.clyberbullying.us/Bullying_and_Cyberbullying_Laws.pdf* (accessed February 28, 2013).

[11] S. Hinduja and J.W. Patchin, *Bullying Beyond the Schoolyard*, p. 5; and J.W. Patchin and S. Hinduja, "Traditional and Nontraditional Bullying Among Youth: A Test of General Strain Theory," *Youth and Society* 43, no. 2 (2011): 727-751.

[12] S. Hinduja and J.W. Patchin, "Cyberbullying: A Review of the Legal Issues Facing Educators," *Preventing School Failure* 55, no. 2 (2010): 1–8.

[13] T.J. Dishion, D.M. Capaldi, and K. Yoerger, "Middle Childhood Antecedents to Progressions in Male Adolescent Substance Use: An Ecological Analysis of Risk and

Protection," *Journal of Adolescent Research*14 (1999): 175-205.

[14] D.L. Haynie, "Delinquent Peers Revisited: Does Network Structure Matter?" *American Journal of Sociology* 106, (2001): 1013-1057.

[15] N.E. Willard, 2010, "School Response to Cyberbullying and Sexting: The Legal Challenges," *Center for Safe and Responsible Internet Use, http://www.embracecivility.org* (accessed January 31, 2013).

[16] S. Hinduja and J.W. Patchin, *Cyberbullying*, p. 1-8.

## Discussion Questions

In every category contained in the survey instrument, the law enforcement executives attending the FBI National Academy rated the relevant law enforcement role lower than that of the school resource officers. Why do you think this was the case?

## Critical Thinking Exercise

Based upon the information and data provided in this article, develop a one page position paper on adopting a new policy on cyberbullying and sexting for school resource officers who have law enforcement responsibilities. You can assume that this particular school or jurisdiction had no previous policy of this nature. Your focus should be on the roles of the different parties, e.g., SROs, detectives, teachers, principals, school counselors, etc.

# OTHER BOOKS BY DR. CENCICH

## THE DEVIL'S GARDEN: A WAR CRIMES INVESTIGATOR'S STORY
### POTOMAC BOOKS

## PROBLEMS IN POLICING
### THE HAGUE PRESS INTERNATIONAL

## OFFENDER MOTIVATION AND VALUES:
## HIGH SPEED ISSUES IN INTERNATIONAL SECURITY
### THE HAGUE PRESS INTERNATIONAL

CPSIA information can be obtained at www.ICGtesting.com
Printed in the USA
BVOW03s1237221114

376253BV00005B/8/P